Inequality and Economic Policies:

Just Tax the Rich?

References for the data:

References for the data can be cross-checked by searching the Internet for the keywords in the text. Otherwise, the author can be contacted through the website findtheflaw.com.

Acknowledgments:

Editing and feedback about text accessibility: Margaret Strubel.

Inequality and Economic Policies: Just Tax the Rich?

(+ A monetary add-on for bridging the gap)

Vincent Lannoye

In memory of my mother.

TABLE OF CONTENTS

Alphabetical Index

Introduction

1. Unyielding Inequality

2. The Government Runs in Circles (Regulations and taxes upset the economy)

Heavy taxation: A political threat
High taxes and the stagflation of the 1970s
Since 1980, cutting tax rates for more(!) fiscal revenues
Cutting tax rates to stem the economic crisis
Cutting tax rates on capital gains for a new economy
The recovery has not lifted low wages
A comeback of high tax rates won't fix inequality

Congress should just pass a new wealth tax, right?
The cash of the rich is gone—tied up in loans or investments
Non-cash assets are difficult to tax
A high wealth tax is unrealistic
Asset confiscation will not revive the economy
Switzerland: Wealth tax success in a low-tax country
Alternative tax on wealth: The capital gains tax
The inescapable tax on wealth: The estate tax
No miracle in plundering the rich

Should the government guide corporations toward better pay and jobs?
The legacy of postwar incremental guidance: A controversial approach
Mandating higher pay can backfire
Tightening the screws: Small corporations should be spared excessive regulation
Deregulation post-1980

US government hesitant to redistribute more
Not too far: Welfare as a potential poverty trap
A negative tax for low-income jobs
Welfare budgets should not overburden the economy
Expanded benefit programs might set others back
The EU: Shrinking benefits over the last decades

Is it just about re-funding education?
The US education budget isn't small
Learning from the experience of other countries
Education is slow to move people up the job ladder

3. Will New Promises Save the Day?

Return of tariffs aimed at raising US wages
Tariffs at the risk of economic disturbance

Technology-driven productivity could create jobs
Productivity gains: Boosting GDP growth and economic well-being
AI could improve productivity across the board

Can AI and Technology Overcome All Obstacles?...........................108

Can AI boost economic growth quickly enough to create jobs?
AI and technology: A unifying force for the Western world?
Technology must also save the climate
Compensating the Global South for green transition efforts

---

4. Monetary Economics, Not Politics

Monetary Changes Have Repeatedly Bypassed Politics....................117

Bibliography

Origin of Illustrations

ALPHABETICAL INDEX

Inequality and Economic Policies: Just Tax the Rich?

(+ A monetary add-on for bridging the gap)

INTRODUCTION

Paying for higher wages ultimately comes down to money—but it is not as simple as it sounds. Creating well-paying jobs in areas like infrastructure, defense, or domestic manufacturing requires significant investment. However, governments face a tough challenge: securing the necessary funds without harming employment. Raising taxes and adding more rules for businesses might seem like obvious answers, but they can backfire by making it harder for companies to hire people.

Blind faith in taxation-based solutions often stems from misunderstandings about how modern money works—often making economic debates more polarized than necessary. Unlike in the past, when money was tied to gold coins, today's money is simply a unit of account—not actual wealth stored in a vault. The idea that governments can simply seize banknotes to solve any problem is misleading. This book will explain this core misconception, which it calls the "money delusion." Understanding the true nature of money is essential for having realistic conversations about economic policy.

Not under any delusion, most economists oppose sweeping tax increases to fund subsidy programs. Instead, they tend to favor targeted tax cuts for low-income workers within the existing market system. The goal is to nudge the job market in the right direction, not to have the government take over entire industries like infrastructure or healthcare.

Yet, economists have not found a reliable way to raise low-income wages while sustaining strong job growth. Their track record in solving major economic problems is mixed. From the Great Depression to the 1970s energy crisis—and now today's persistent inequality—mainstream economics has often struggled to deliver effective solutions, as discussed in *The History of Money for Understanding Economics* (see the final chapter).

That said, solutions are not out of reach. Other approaches may be worth exploring.

Part 1

UNYIELDING INEQUALITY

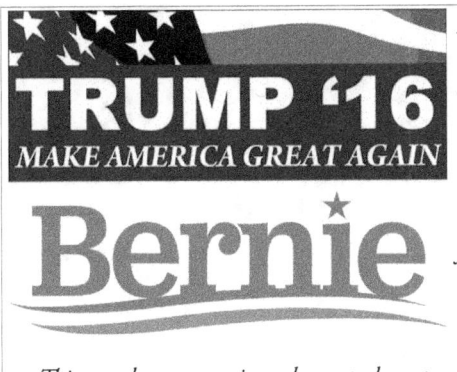

Persistent low wages continue to afflict workers in the US and the EU, even as others benefit from economic growth. This gap has fueled political polarization, with some turning to the far left, blaming the rich, and others moving toward right-wing movements, blaming foreigners. In the US, this shift has elevated once-outsider figures like Trump and Sanders, leaving traditional politicians behind.

This trend poses a serious threat to long-term stability, as political leaders continue to fall short of delivering meaningful wage growth. Disillusioned voters may turn to increasingly extreme alternatives—some of whom could seek to consolidate power or gradually impose authoritarian rule.

Preventing this outcome requires a clear grasp of the economic roots of wage stagnation. Simply redistributing wealth risks backfiring—hurting the economy and increasing unemployment. The problem is not a lack of political will but the absence of straightforward economic solutions. Today's wage struggles may stem from outdated economic thinking, rigid monetary systems, and a regulatory framework in need of reform. Moving forward will demand fresh ideas in economics, macroeconomics, and monetary policy.

Low-Income Workers Are Feeling the Pain

Decades of stagnant income for the lower middle class

The economic dissatisfaction among the lower-income middle class is understandable, as many have faced stagnant wages for decades. The steady wage growth that characterized the post-war period largely came to an end for the middle class in the 1970s. Since then, many low-income workers have seen their wages decline in real terms, forcing them to live paycheck to paycheck.

This trend is troubling, especially since the economy has grown during the same period. It means that most of the benefits have gone to the upper middle class and top earners, increasing the income gap. The following sections examine the widening gap between those who have and those who do not.

Persistent inequality threatens social cohesion. A society divided by economic frustration cannot endure indefinitely, as such pressures often spark political instability. These divisions can fuel domestic unrest and even geopolitical tensions, with nations or groups seeking scapegoats for economic hardship. The consequences could be severe.

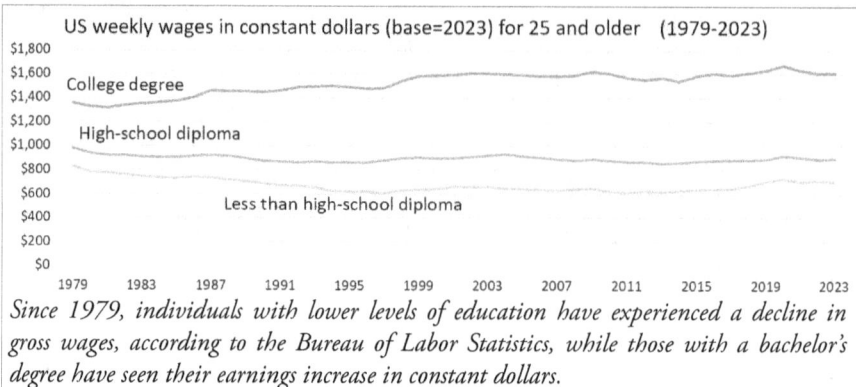

Since 1979, individuals with lower levels of education have experienced a decline in gross wages, according to the Bureau of Labor Statistics, while those with a bachelor's degree have seen their earnings increase in constant dollars.

For many, college is not a viable path from the lowest to the highest income bracket. Numerous students either do not finish high school, struggle with college entrance requirements, or must enter the workforce immediately due to financial constraints. This trend is evident both in the US and globally. Even in countries where financial aid is available, not everyone chooses to pursue higher education, and US college graduation rates are comparable to those of other Western nations.

Stagnant wages despite economic booms

Despite periods of economic growth—such as the Reagan-era expansion in the 1980s, the dot-com boom of the 1990s, and the housing boom of the 2000s—many workers have not seen significant wage increases. Even when unemployment declined and demand for labor should have driven wages up, lower-middle-class earnings remained stagnant.

In theory, all wages should have risen during periods of strong economic growth. But for the past 50 years, wages for lower-income workers have barely improved—contrary to economists' expectations. Although there was some recovery after 2015, these gains were short-lived, as wages declined again following the COVID-19 crisis. After decades of stagnation, a full recovery remains a long-term challenge.

Income growth concentrated at the top

Since the 1970s, OECD data shows that high earners have captured most of the economic expansion's benefits through wages. The upper tier of the middle class—those earning twice the median income—has fared better than the lower middle class, which earns less than two-thirds of the median and has seen little to no financial progress.

The concentration of economic gains among the rich, combined with stagnant wages for others, has fueled frustration among lower-income workers. Many feel stuck in a cycle of financial stagnation while watching the wealthiest continue to accumulate more. This growing disparity is driving louder calls for change.

In technical terms, income distribution is often measured through Gross Domestic Product ("GDP") growth. GDP represents the total value of all goods and services produced in a country, calculated as the sum of consumption, investment, government spending, and net exports. In essence, GDP reflects the nation's income, which is primarily distributed as wages before being allocated to profits and dividends, as reported to the IRS. Both GDP figures and IRS wage statistics are publicly available.

Drivers of wage stagnation among low-income workers

The stagnation of low-income wages stems primarily from insufficient competition among employers seeking low-skill labor. Economists point to several key factors driving this trend:

• Automation: The displacement of workers by machines, robots and computers is considered a primary cause of wage stagnation. Automation allows fewer workers and administrative staff to produce more efficiently, reducing the need for additional labor. In some cases, entire job categories have been eliminated as machines take over tasks previously performed by humans.

• Globalization: The expansion of global trade has sent jobs to low-wage countries, increased competition from foreign imports, and redirected investments abroad. These factors collectively put downward pressure on wages. However, while globalization affects wage levels, automation has had a greater impact.

• Declining bargaining power: An oversupply of labor and limited job opportunities make it particularly difficult for younger workers to enter the workforce and advance up the wage ladder. At the same time, the decline of labor unions has further reduced workers' ability to negotiate higher pay.

• Regulation and taxation: Economists, particularly free-market advocates, argue that excessive regulations and taxation can disrupt economic growth. Regulations increase corporate costs through compliance requirements, legal fees, and engineering expenses, resulting in companies abandoning less profitable projects and cutting jobs. Taxation reduces disposable income for consumers and investors, limiting business expansion and hiring because demand for goods and services remains constrained.

Economic shocks and job losses have escalated tensions over time

Following the post-war economic boom and a period of near-full employment, mass unemployment emerged in the 1970s. This instability, along with the threat of job losses during downturns, fueled growing discontent.

With each economic crisis—such as those in 1974, 1982, 1991, 2001, and 2008—many workers lost their jobs, depleted their savings, and struggled to recover even when the economy improved. Even those who retained their jobs often faced uncertainty, as fears of layoffs, particularly in low-skill sectors, created ongoing financial insecurity.

It took decades for the official U-3 unemployment rate to recover and consistently fall below the 5% mark seen in the late 1960s. In fact, it was only after 2015 that this rate remained steadily below 5%. This rate (of "unemployed people actively looking for a job") is measured by the BLS (US Bureau of Labor Statistics).

In reality, despite the recovery of this U-3 figure, many remain affected by joblessness, as other indicators show:

• Other unemployment rates unveil graver underemployment than the official rate. For example, the U-6—also from the BLS—is double the U-3 rate. The U-6 is the U-3 plus people discouraged by job rejections, and postponing their job search until better times, and thus excluded from the official unemployment rate.

• The "labor force participation rate" in 2017 discloses a low 63% of active workers compared with the population of working age. This figure is the lowest since 1977.

• The disparity between age groups is another disturbing figure. The employment of the category 25-54 years old—the main pool of post-college work skills of the future—stagnates around 80% despite the recovery. Only the 55 and older have progressed since the 2008 crisis, while the 16-24 age group has declined.

• Other disparities exist about states, counties, age groups, race, or sex, etc. They can trigger social tensions.

The full employment and strong wages of the post-war era are long gone. Along with them, the decline in income inequality that began with the "Great Compression" of the early 1940s came to an end in the 1970s. Since then, recurrent unemployment and job insecurity have disproportionately affected low-skill workers.

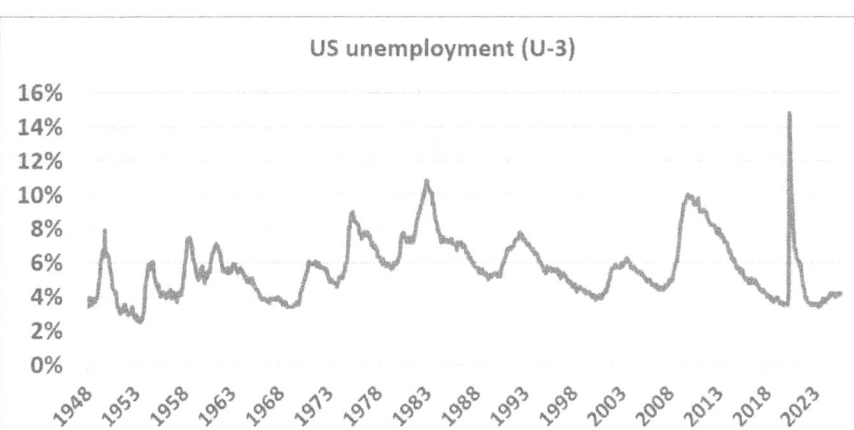

Since the 1970s, crises have hit low-skill workers harder, with unemployment reaching higher levels and falling more slowly than in the postwar decades. This pattern was evident during the oil shocks of 1974 and 1979, the Gulf War recession of 1990, the dot-com bust of 2001, the subprime crisis of 2008, and, most recently, the Covid-19 crisis of 2020.

Welfare benefits primarily the poorest

The government can positively influence low wages by lowering tax rates and providing free welfare services or in-kind benefits for specific low-income household expenses. After all, it is take-home income that truly matters to individuals, although workers also pay attention to their gross wages.

Such governmental actions have been minimal in recent decades, more like a band-aid on wages, as the government struggles to find money to support low-income households while still balancing its budget. The difficulty lies in transferring money from the rich to the poor without destroying jobs.

Since the 1980s, government transfers and free services have only helped raise the income of the lowest-earning 20% of workers by approximately 20%, as shown in the table below (source: cbo.gov). Many of these workers remain heavily reliant on welfare programs to maintain a basic standard of living.

These benefits do not extend to middle-class workers above the welfare eligibility thresholds. As a result, the broader middle class has seen little to no benefit from such income transfers:

Transfers over wages	Lowest Quintile	Second Quintile	Middle Quintile	Fourth Quintile	Top Quintile
1980s	14.2%	-2.8%	-1.4%	-1.3%	-0.2%
1990s	20.8%	-0.9%	-3.1%	-2.1%	-0.2%
2000s	18.9%	1.4%	-2.7%	-1.3%	-0.1%
2010s	21.2%	4%	-2%	-1%	-0.2%

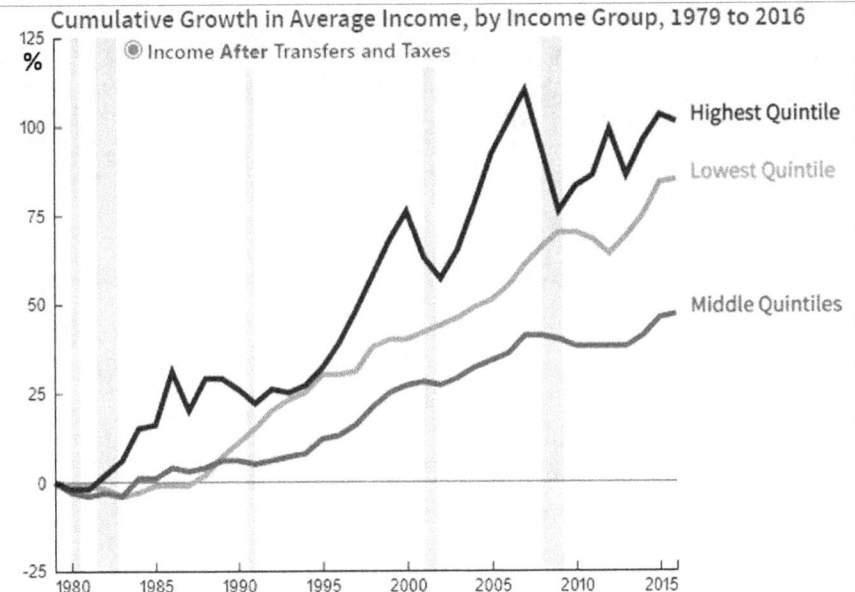

Cumulative Growth in Average Income, by Income Group, 1979 to 2016

According to the Congressional Budget Office (cob.gov), incomes of households have risen after accounting for transfers and taxes. These household incomes include not just net wages, but also other sources such as social security, interests, dividends, or negative taxes.

Nevertheless, the specter of inequality persists. First, a 75% increase can represent a few thousand dollars for the lowest quintile, but may represent several million dollars for the highest quintile. Second, people looking at individual income have a point: their individual hourly wages, not just their post-tax household income, should keep up with other wages no matter what, and the fruits of the GDP growth should not just fall on the rich.

Unrelenting global income inequality

Many countries have yet to achieve an optimal balance in income distribution, as reflected in the Gini index of the World Bank. European nations may point to better outcomes in reducing inequalities with their social policies, but often at the expense of long-term technological investment and adequate military capacity.

Given the lack of a universally accepted model, most nations remain as perplexed as divided about solutions to inequality and exclusion. The following section will explore various approaches, assessing their potential merits and pitfalls.

The Impact of Additional Costs on Household Budgets

Housing costs deepen inequality

Beyond the problem of stagnant wages, low-income workers devote a high percentage of their income to rent or mortgage payments, while wealthier individuals spend much less proportionally. Worse, housing and rental costs have increased faster than inflation since the late 1990s. This one-two punch of stagnant wages and expensive housing has hit low-income individuals particularly hard.

Those who relocate to cities with greater employment opportunities are often severely affected. Job centers are typically located in areas where low-income workers are consistently priced out of housing by higher-paid professionals in fields such as technology or finance, as in San Francisco or New York.

In rural areas, declining property values hinder homeowners from selling and relocating to cities with better job prospects. Those who do attempt to move face a difficult trade-off: selling their homes at low prices while confronting steep urban housing costs. This disparity further complicates relocation for workers seeking improved financial stability.

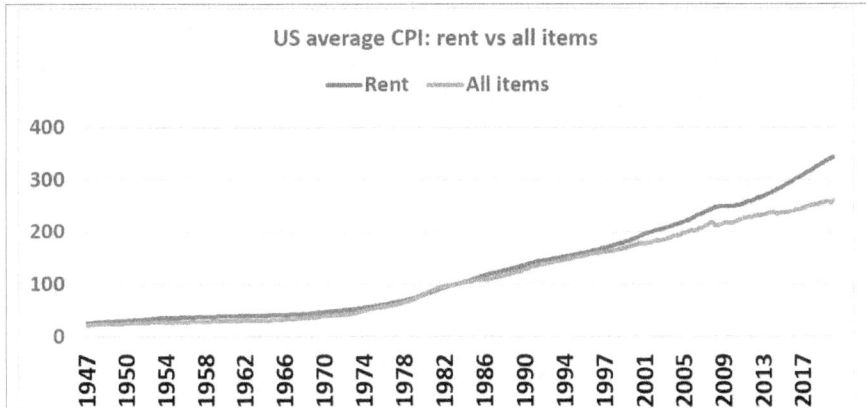

Since the late 1990s, rental prices have risen faster than most other goods and services. The main drivers include population growth, migration to cities with strong job markets, and a shortage of new construction. This trend is clear in the Consumer Price Index (CPI) for rent compared with the overall CPI.

For low-income individuals, the impact is a double squeeze: wages barely keep up with inflation, while rent eats up more of their budget.

Rising healthcare costs are adding pressure

The cost of health insurance has risen significantly over the past decades. This surge in healthcare costs can be attributed to various factors, including workforce shortages and the expansion of advanced but expensive high-tech care. Overall, healthcare costs climbed from 7% of US GDP in the 1970s to more than 15% after 2000.

Ultimately, people must bear the burden of national healthcare expenditures. These costs are currently distributed through an insurance system in which premiums are calculated per person, per area, and per age, but not proportionally to income. Even when subsidies are available, they usually do not offset the steep rise in premiums. Rising healthcare costs worsen inequality by draining a disproportionately large share of the personal budgets of low-income households.

The financial burden of college education

For many young people, college is seen as a pathway out of low-wage work. Yet in the US, the cost of higher education is substantial. Expenses include tuition, housing, food, and other essentials, along with the opportunity cost of lost income from not working during college years. Over the past few decades, studies have shown that these costs have risen faster than inflation, placing a heavy burden on families supporting their children's education and on students who take on debt to earn their degrees.

In the US, financial aid for students remains a controversial issue. Some argue that middle-class taxpayers should not have to subsidize higher education for wealthier families, while others point out that grants and low-cost community colleges still provide some relief.

In contrast, student financial aid in the European Union is generally less contentious, as college costs are often covered by taxpayer funding. However, despite this financial support, college graduation rates in the EU are not significantly higher than those in the US.

Widening Wealth Inequality

Growth of the stock market for the rich

While the middle class struggles, the wealth of the richest continues to grow, in addition to their comfortable income from wages, interest, and dividends. Their portfolios include assets such as cash, real estate, Treasury bonds, corporate bonds, and stocks.

Their wealth has expanded particularly through the stock market. Over recent decades, this growth has been fueled by GDP expansion and declining interest rates, and it can be tracked using measures like the "Brock Value" or the "Buffett Indicator" (both explained in detail online).

Similarly, their real estate wealth has surged with skyrocketing housing prices in economic hubs, driven by migration from rural areas to cities and from the Rust Belt to the Sun Belt. Housing prices also climbed as record-low interest rates encouraged buyers to overbid, given the prospect of cheaper monthly mortgage payments. Once again, it was not hard work but external factors that boosted landlords' wealth.

This accumulation of wealth is well documented, as shown in Forbes' *Billionaires List* and in academic studies that compile data on real estate and stock holdings from public records or directly from the billionaires themselves.

The growing wealth of the rich often sparks anger, with critics denouncing "tax cuts for the wealthy" as during the "Fight Oligarchy" tour. However, polls—such as those from Pew Research—suggest that most people are not seeking to strip the rich of their wealth in exchange for handouts or charity. Economic inequality is not a top priority for most Americans. The middle class is less concerned with punishing the wealthy and more focused on their own financial security. What people want are better wages, which have stagnated for decades. This sentiment is also reflected in the fact that many of them support Donald Trump, who is known for his billionaire status. Inequality, then, is best understood as a problem of low wages—not simply wealth at the top.

Limited investment opportunities for the middle class

For the middle class, wealth building is a different story. Many struggle to invest in real estate or in the stock market due to their limited incomes and rising costs. Even during economic downturns—when housing investments might become more affordable—job instability often prevents them from securing mortgages. As a result, financial opportunities for the lower half of the population remain severely constrained.

To provide perspective, the bottom half of the country holds a minimal stake in the stock market. In contrast, the wealthiest 10% of Americans own a record 89% of all US stocks. On top of it, this privileged group frequently reinvest its dividends utilizing lawful tax havens, thereby bypassing tax liabilities.

Savings accounts offer little relief. Bank interest rates, which were as high as 8% in the 1980s, dropped to around 1% after the 2008 financial crisis. Although interest rates increased after 2021, inflation also surged, eroding the purchasing power of low-wage workers.

For those living in small towns, property values have remained stagnant, offering little opportunity for home equity growth. This financial stagnation has left many feeling trapped in economic uncertainty and limited upward mobility.

Future Challenges in Technology and Climate Change

The impact of high-tech and AI on employment

The rise of artificial intelligence (AI) in the coming years could further strain low-wage jobs. AI is expected to speed up automation across industries—including robotics and self-driving vehicles—posing a threat to both job availability and wages for low-skill workers, from factory employees to truck drivers. Economic studies suggest this trend may keep wages low for the lower segments of the workforce. At the same time, technological progress is unlikely to slow—especially given its crucial role in maintaining the United States' economic strength and military competitiveness.

Job insecurity may not be limited to low-skill roles. Many white-collar positions could also be affected, as AI-powered software begins to replace clerical workers and even some software developers. New graduates are already locked out of entry-level jobs—positions like junior programmer or assistant designer—while retraining in trades such as welding or electrical work remains out of reach for many. That leaves much of the younger generation trapped in low-quality jobs with little upside, underemployment, or outright displacement, often with lower wages, while seasoned engineers largely hold their ground.

On the other hand, some believe that rapid technological progress could actually strengthen the job market instead of simply eliminating jobs. This surprising shift in the economic landscape is explored later in the book.

The projected costs of the green transition

The transition to a clean energy infrastructure will require massive investment, and those costs must ultimately be borne by someone. The central question is: who will pay for electric vehicles, batteries, nuclear power, and green energy?

In the best-case scenario, global temperatures rise only gradually, while breakthroughs in green technology—such as advances in battery storage or nuclear fusion—deliver affordable energy that outcompetes oil and coal. At the same time, carbon taxes ensure that fossil fuels do not undercut green energy.

In the worst-case scenario, global warming accelerates while the transition to clean energy remains costly. This would disproportionately affect low-income households, since energy accounts for a large share of their budgets. Economic studies suggest that rising energy costs would hit these households hardest, making the shift to green energy a significant financial challenge. Subsidies can help ease the burden, but they cannot fully offset it without risking reduced incentives for the transition.

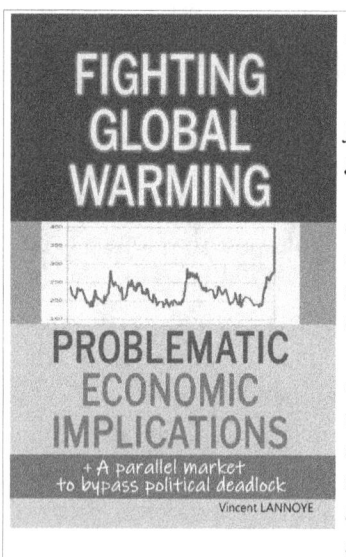

Inequality and global warming are the two armies launching a pincer movement on a bemused society.

Without inequalities, carbon taxing could hit fossil energy as the united people would accept the green transition without political backlash.

Without global warming, economic growth absolved from carbon regulations could create jobs, increase wages, and start reducing inequalities, within a less disputed business model powered by cheap energy.

As background for the following pages, another book on global warming overlaps with this one to warn against demagogic solutions. That book argues there is only one real hope for containing global warming: breakthroughs in technology. New green technologies could replace hydrocarbons, while other innovations might push economic growth above 3% annually—since only such rapid growth can create jobs, raise wages, and begin to reduce inequality.

Does it all depend on fantastic technological breakthroughs? Well, one can think out of the box. One last book refers to a new monetary or macroeconomic idea at the end of this present book.

Part 2

THE GOVERNMENT

RUNS IN CIRCLES

(REGULATIONS AND TAXES

UPSET THE ECONOMY)

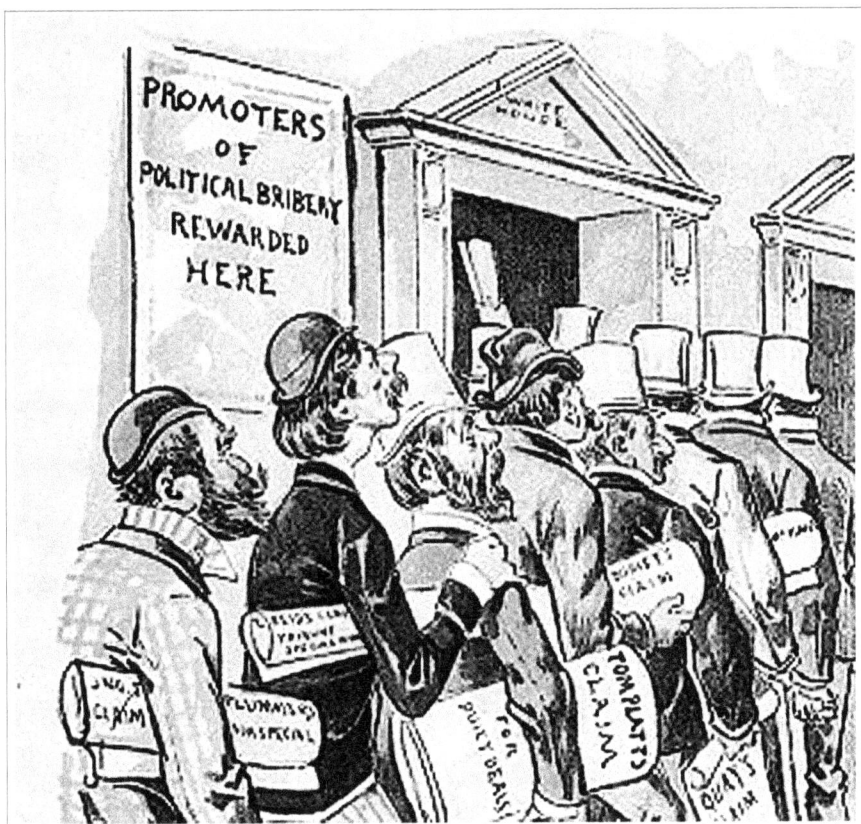

Are wealthy lobbyists bribing politicians to avoid action on low wages? Not exactly. The issue is more complex, as the next section will explain. Governments struggle because economists haven't found a reliable way to raise wages for lower- and middle-income workers without risking job losses. Many doubt that government policies alone can lift wages without also causing unemployment. Instead, they often suggest leaving most of the work to market forces.

No, Borrowing Cannot Bankroll Everything

Splurging through borrowing to solve it all?

Given the pressing need to address inequality, could endless borrowing be justified to fund free services? Shouldn't banks be compelled to extend generous loans at low interest rates, with repayment terms stretching across centuries? Wouldn't it make sense for governments to adopt such a financial strategy to promote social equity and provide long-term solutions to pressing challenges?

Alternatively, the government could bypass private banks and have the Treasury raise funds by issuing "*bonds*"—loan contracts that pay periodic interest. These bonds would be sold to the public in the "*bond market*," a network of brokers who buy and resell bonds. The "*Federal Reserve System*"—commonly known as the "*Fed*"—could step in and purchase large amounts of these bonds to stabilize the Treasury market, as it often does. Such funding methods were used during World War I, World War II, the 2008 financial crisis, and the 2020 COVID-19 crisis. At those times, Congress approved substantial borrowing to finance stimulus packages without raising taxes, supporting projects that created jobs. Isn't it time to embrace extensive borrowing in one form or another?

Borrowing like crazy leads to inflation

Borrowing multiplies money

Contemporary monetary creation evolved through centuries of financial trial and error, as illustrated in the following picture. Today, it begins with the requests of borrowers. To meet these requests, banks are authorized to create money "out of thin air" by crediting most of the loan amount to borrowers' accounts. In this sense, monetary creation is initiated by borrowers rather than solely by bankers' unilateral decisions. However, this process carries risks: if a borrower defaults, the bank must absorb the loss—typically by using profits earned from interest on other performing loans to cover the shortfall.

It is important to note that the money supply originates from borrowing through bank loans. Borrowers then spend this newly created money on goods, services, raw materials, machinery, and labor. These resources empower borrowers to produce, sell, keep some profits and finally pay back their loan. This process constitutes a critical aspect of the broader economic cycle, putting financial institutions at the core of the economy.

A short summary about "monetary creation":

For thousands of years, the ounce of gold or silver was the basis of money, with a ratio of roughly 15 ounces of silver equating to 1 ounce of gold. Monetary creation or "money supply" came from mining and coining precise fractions of ounces of silver or gold. Although banking did exist, its primary function was limited to loaning the precious coins in deposit at the bank. Banks could have 100 coins from depositors, and the same bank could loan 50 coins, whose depositors were unlikely to withdraw soon.

Around 1700, monetary creation started to stray away from mining gold and silver. At that time, bankers learned magically to loan 110 coins with only 100 coins in their vaults, which was a true monetary creation of 10 coins! How did they do it? In fact, borrowers would not withdraw 110 coins, but instead they would withdraw 110 coin-equivalents in the form of the new paper banknotes recently invented. Borrowers would accept withdrawing their loans in banknotes, because these banknotes were convertible into precious coins at the bank's counter. These banknotes could return for coin-conversion, but only after payment in a few days or even weeks, as customers would start trusting and keeping these banknotes. This trust enabled the bank to issue banknotes equivalent to 110% of its coin reserves in order to earn more interest.

Over the course of the 18th and 19th centuries, monetary creation has gradually shifted from minting gold or silver coins, to borrowing banknotes convertible into coins... until the suspension after 1930 of coin-convertibility in most countries.

Today, money is created through bank loans, as by everyone who has a credit card (as in the picture). Each time a credit card is used to pay for a purchase, money is created in this credit account. Of course, money is destroyed when the credit card account is paid back, but other credit card users will borrow simultaneously to sustain and potentially augment the overall money supply. For more detailed information, refer to the book "The History of Money for Understanding Economics," mentioned on the last page.

Money multiplication: Tempting and dangerous

Of course, rapid money multiplications have been attempted throughout history—whether through the debasement of coins, the printing of banknotes, or unrestrained borrowing—from Roman emperors to the 1970s and even today in corrupt countries. For centuries, demagogues have borrowed recklessly, either to cling to power or under the pretense of addressing global challenges.

In reality, a dramatic increase in money creation by governments—whether through a string of loans from private banks or through massive public loans from a central bank to its government—has never been a panacea for resolving economic problems. On the contrary, such endless borrowing has consistently disrupted the economy through inflation and, in some cases, has even doomed entire economies as they slid into hyperinflation.

If an immense treasure or even a mountain of gold would be found, could the government distribute gold ingots to the people and all the problems of global warming and inequality would be solved? Certainly not. In reality, the price of gold would simply collapse.

Similarly, if a vast amount of loans were coerced from banks, flooding the government coffers and people's pockets with endless dollars, it would not resolve issues such as low wages and inequality. Instead, the value of money would collapse due to a phenomenon known as inflation or even hyper-inflation.

In case of money dump in circulation: prices spike

Excessive borrowing can dangerously expand the money supply. This uncontrolled borrowing multiplies banknotes, which are then used in payments by the government, corporations, and private borrowers. The likely outcome is a mechanical rise in prices that unfolds as follows:

• Circulation Surge: Money enters circulation as it is spent by corporations and individuals who borrow or draw from their savings. It then flows among suppliers, workers, civil servants, and retirees—who all become consumers. With cash in hand, these customers throng the stores.

• Inventory Depletion: Producers and sellers see their inventory decreasing. They can't replenish their stocks quickly due to production inertia, delivery delays, or a lack of trained workers. To preserve stock for their best customers, they look for other ways to adjust.

• Price Adjustments: With low inventory levels, neither producers nor sellers can satisfy every customer—even with alternative products or brands. They begin selling without offering the usual discounts, which effectively causes prices to rise. In modern retail chains with displayed prices, marketing departments also respond to low stock levels by canceling weekly promotions and increasing prices. If low inventories affect a wide range of products, a broad spectrum of prices will rise—if not all.

In summary, a rapid multiplication of money in circulation sets off a chain of events that increases all prices across every sector and retail environment.

Bargaining in Arab countries is very instructive. If one has any doubt about the price hike linked to expanding money supply, he can show the camel owner a bundle of banknotes before negotiating the price of the camel ride.

Prolonged price rises characterized as inflation

Prices continuously rise when producers see their capacity to restock goods consistently outstripped by consumer demand fueled by cash in hand. As money multiplication continues, prices increase month after month, year after year. This phenomenon of generalized and prolonged rise of prices is called "*inflation*" or sometimes "*price inflation.*"

It is important to specify that the surge of a single price does not define inflation. An isolated price may increase from occasional, climatic or seasonal factors, while a simultaneous decline in another price can offset the effect. Instead, inflation is the measure of the average rise of all prices across the entire spectrum of goods and services.

It should also be noted that a sudden panic can increase money in circulation when buyers empty their savings and rush to clear out store shelves. This general surge in prices is not considered inflation, as it is not persistent and prices may stabilize later on.

Lasting high inflation would drag the economy down

Savers, such as retirees or those with future spending targets, will see the purchasing power of their savings trimmed by inflation. They will realize it as their savings yields struggle to keep pace with the climbing prices of food, utilities or their dream purchase. They are rarely compensated by high interests when borrowing rules are lax, as it was the case during the 1970s. They will find themselves compelled to curtail their consumption of unessential goods and services.

Not all workers receive raises that keep pace with inflation, especially when job security concerns loom large—particularly in companies hurt by weak demand from savers. As a result, many cut back on spending, further worsening the economic outlook.

Corporations and businesses will grapple with the challenges posed by inflation, which creates uncertainty in future demand patterns due to dwindling savings. As a result, factories may reduce output and inventory to mitigate the risk of selling products at a loss due to possible weak demand. This cautious approach often involves furloughs and hiring freezes to align with scaled-back production.

Inflation's disproportionate impact on the poor

Inflation hits the lower middle class hardest. They face rising expenses and have limited financial resources to withstand persistent price increases, particularly in food and housing. Their savings lose value, while securing wage increases becomes more difficult—especially during an inflation-driven slowdown. As a result, many in this group are forced to cut back on spending, which can further weaken the economy.

The poorest individuals fare somewhat better, since their welfare benefits are indexed to inflation. But this support does not extend to the middle class, which earns too much to qualify for assistance yet still struggles with rising costs.

By contrast, the wealthy are better positioned to shield themselves from inflation. With access to financial expertise, they can invest in inflation-resistant assets such as gold, real estate, or stocks.

Inflation could feed on itself and get out of control

Borrowing let loose through accommodating interest rates and regulations to fix all the problems of the world would favor borrowers, as their repayments are eased by inflation. Borrowers could even borrow, buy, wait for inflation to drive up their value, resell at a higher price, pay back the fixed loan amount with its meager interests, while cashing in the price discrepancy between transactions. This borrowing on steroids, with a continual influx of new loans, would inject shot after shot of banknotes in circulation and worsen inflation.

Long-term investments are penalized by inflation, which makes forecasting of upcoming costs uncertain and demand of savers unsure. The least profitable projects end up being declined, as investors dread a repayment hit by climbing costs and shrinking demand. Instead, investors prefer unproductive placements such as real estate, stock market, or commodities.

At that point, the negative spillover of inflation begins to seriously derail the economy with job cuts of idle workers as a consequence of discontinuing low-return projects unable to keep up with inflation.

Then, the risk exists for inflation to feed on itself with a dangerous spiral of always more banknotes, less output and less jobs.

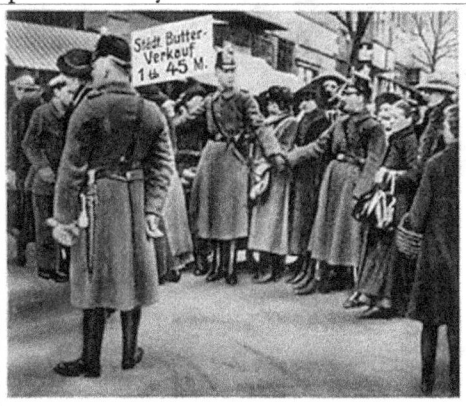

In January 1922, Germany entered a period of "*hyperinflation*," marked by extremely rapid price increases. The money supply ballooned through borrowing, while the availability of goods paradoxically shrank. After all, why work hard to produce if savings could not be preserved at a stable value? As incentives to work collapsed, production shifted to meeting only short-term needs. National output fell sharply, and the entire country grew poorer. In the end, multiplying money only meant longer lines for food—and paying 45 million marks for a pound of butter. This episode underscores that real wealth lies in tangible goods, not in the symbolic illusion of paper banknotes.

Since the 1980s: Borrowing under surveillance

Containing money supply to curb inflation

The sobering experience of the 1970s, with its stubborn inflation, changed the minds of economists. They stopped believing that an economic slowdown should be countered with ever more borrowing and public spending, as had been done during World War II and the postwar era—especially since money could be created easily through borrowing after gold convertibility for the American public ended in 1934.

Economists came to assume that a major cause of economic slowdowns was inflation fueled by excessive borrowing. Implicitly, they accepted that output would normally remain strong, since workers were ready to roll up their sleeves and corporations were eager to expand production quickly to capture market share. Since then, this view has held significant sway among economists, who generally agree that inflation is, above all, a monetary phenomenon tied to loose borrowing rules.

With this shift in thinking, policymakers accepted that borrowing must be contained, even when pursued for worthy goals such as stimulating job creation or funding welfare programs to reduce poverty. Strict oversight is essential to keep the money supply from spiraling out of control.

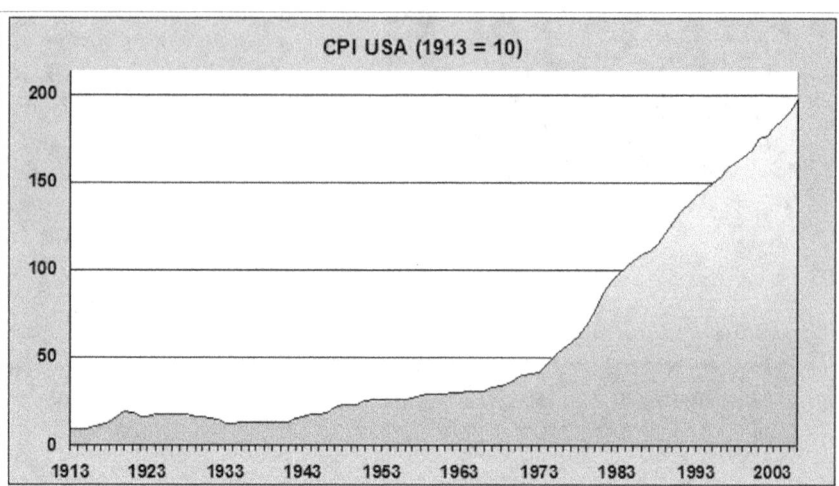

In the 1970s, the US was confronted with an upswing in inflation (as visible in the picture with inflation measured by the Consumer Price Index). Inflation was a new phenomenon. People witnessed the purchasing power of their savings eroded by inflation. The unemployment rate was climbing. The economic growth was stuttering. The post-war economic policies—inspired by the economist John Keynes and known as "Keynesianism"—were challenged by inflation. The continuously low interest rates and recurrent public deficit to boost governmental spending were backfiring with inflation.

Around 1980, inflation became the main economic focus. The alternative ideas of the "monetarist" economists, spearheaded by the economist Milton Friedman, were finally taken seriously. Their monetarist ideas came to amend Keynesianism, with the central analysis that the government often triggers the economic instability, more than corporations inclined to grow their market shares, and not always overcautious as believed by Keynesianism.

From then on, the strategy shifted from high-taxes-with-government-spending to tax-cuts-with-less-government, while targeting low inflation. In other words, the spending of the borrowing was entrusted to the private sector. It was hoped that money and borrowing in hands of people and corporations would lift the economy, not borrowing controlled by the government's bureaucracy.

Borrowing under the scrutiny of an independent Fed

In 1977, Congress revised the Federal Reserve's mandate to fight inflation, though it took several years before it was effectively implemented. The Fed is now charged with promoting maximum employment, stable prices, and moderate long-term interest rates. The Fed has different tools to comply with its mandate:

• The Fed must slow the pace of borrowing to regulate the money supply and ensure that inflation stays near 2% per year, as measured by the Consumer Price Index (CPI) published by the Bureau of Labor Statistics. To do so, the Fed aims at raising interest rates, which should discourage borrowing, limit the money supply and muzzle inflation. Specifically, the Fed influences short-term interest rates—technically called the short-term *"yield"*—on the bond market by selling or buying short-term bonds at a desired interest rate. The Fed has the dollars to buy, stash and resell bonds, as it is allowed by Congress to create money ex nihilo like any bank, as explained previously. The Fed's desired short-term rate will compel corporate bond sellers to compete with a similar interest rate if they want to find a buyer. Indirectly, all mid-term and long-term banking interest rates will align accordingly. Banks will be unable to offer loans at much higher interest rates than those available in the bond market, as other financial entities can issue bonds and use the proceeds to provide loans at competitive rates.

• The Fed may reduce its interest rates to encourage borrowing and sustain consumption during an economic slowdown. In case of a banking crisis, the Fed may even provide emergency loans to rescue institutions that did not trigger the crisis, but always with collateral assets left at the Fed. This helps to ensure that banks remain solvent and able to lend to businesses and consumers.

• The Fed must be impartial to support the economy. The Fed must maintain political neutrality and avoid using monetary policy to manipulate interest rates for partisan political purposes, and never helping one political party or another win an election. The *"Fed"* is an independent Central Bank that is not fully controlled by the government. It is not permitted to lend money directly to the government. This is a common practice among Central Banks around the world, especially since credit facilities from Central Banks to governments have been banned in most countries since the 1980s. To ensure its neutrality, the Fed was granted relative independence from the government, with its board members elected for 14 years (thus, escaping a systematic demotion with each new US President), except for the President of the Board nominated for only 5 years. The Fed operates under a clear legal framework, which includes the obligation to reject funding for an overspending populist government.

Before considering a surge in borrowing, it is important to understand that banknotes are like certificates attesting of "rights-to-consume" that should only be granted after the completion of "efforts-to-produce."

Individuals can get an advance or a loan of rights-to-consume, provided they repay it soon. This is possible as long as others are saving their rights-to-consume for later and they keep producing more than they currently consume. Obviously, the volume of borrowed rights-to-consume must match the output of efforts-to-produce intended to be saved.

If a government, for populist reasons, forces the overissuance of these rights and their free distribution, merchants will inevitably observe an accelerated depletion of their inventories beyond their replenishment rate. Rapidly, the rights-to-consume would depreciate, mirroring the currency collapse of a failed state.

Only during a crisis can the government borrow and spend rights-to-consume when people are too scared to spend their own rights-to-consume. As the crisis subsides and confidence returns, this borrowing must be phased out so that individuals can once again rely on their own rights-to-consume.

The Treasury's borrowing on the bond market

To address the deficit between tax revenue and public expenditures, the Treasury can sell its bonds, but exclusively to the public of private corporations and private citizens within the "***bond market.***" This market is a network of brokers who buy and resell on behalf of a diverse clientele including individuals, corporations, banks, and foreign entities. It is important to note that private banks can purchase Treasury bonds, but they do so using funds from deposits, not from heavily regulated loan accounts that are credited with money out-of-thin-air.

The first reason for Treasury bonds is for banning bank loans credited with money out-of-thin-air from the Fed which must maintain its political impartiality. Such a method of public borrowing from the Fed would be equivalent to a bank loan out-of-thin-air, which is banned, as seen previously. In the same spirit, the Fed can only create money to engage in bond transactions on the open market—never directly with the Treasury—with the sole objective of ensuring economic stability. It is vital that the Fed refuses to shovel cash to the government's Treasury, in order to clamp down on distribution of free money before upcoming elections, even if this limitless funding stems from laudable goals, such as mitigating inequalities. Any borrowing spree has inherent risks of economic destabilization. It cannot be overlooked.

The second reason for selling bonds is to enable the bond market to distinguish and reject junk bonds issued by an inept government. This mechanism ensures a layer of accountability and transparency, fostering a balanced economic landscape. It means that the bond market must have trust in the government to buy its Treasury bonds. The same happens for states, counties and cities selling their own municipal bonds. Obviously, the same is true for previous bond issues which can quickly lose value if a government suddenly changes its course toward insanity.

The rejection criteria of the lenders is based on an assessment considering three main elements:

• Risk of loan default: Lenders will examine the country's economic strategy and its prospective ability to fulfill its bond repayment obligations. Also, lenders pay scrupulous attention to a nation's level of indebtedness. This factor becomes paramount when a nation, already burdened by debt, is hit by a global crisis. Such an accident can severely diminish the country's tax revenue, rendering it incapable of meeting its interest obligations.

• Risk associated with the currency denomination of bonds: Another limit of borrowing is the chronic weakness of a foreign currency, often correlated with the recurrent elections of demagogic leaders. In this context, the bond market will be as vigilant as the currency market. The bond market may demand that bonds be issued in strong dollars or euros.

• The interest rate on the bonds: investors scrutinize the interest rate on bonds, comparing the yield with those of other bonds available in the market. In some instances, particular bonds must offer a much higher return than other bonds to compensate for the inherent risks.

Public deficits are tolerable if they don't impede growth

A small amount of public borrowing is built into most government budgets. A public deficit is generally acceptable if it amounts to only a few percent of GDP and remains smaller than the rate of GDP growth, which implies a declining debt-to-GDP ratio. For example, a 2% public deficit coupled with a 3% growth rate results in a shrinking debt-to-GDP ratio.

Governments should avoid expanding borrowing beyond the generally sustainable deficit level of 2–3% of GDP, except in times of crisis. During such crises, borrowing is preferable to raising taxes, since higher taxes in a downturn discourage spending and investment, weakening the economy and delaying recovery. By contrast, a faster recovery increases fiscal revenues sooner and reduces the deficit more quickly than if the crisis were prolonged.

Never should a permanent large-scale public deficit be allowed, even with the intention of creating large numbers of well-paid jobs to build hospitals and schools. Such a policy would only expand bureaucracy and generate inflationary pressures that could derail the economy.

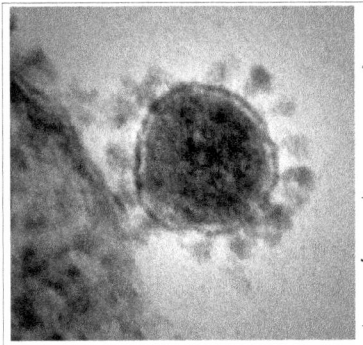

Yes, the government must step in during emergencies like the Covid crisis, but the same recipe can't fund a flurry of public projects.

During the Covid lockdown, emergency funding helped the people and businesses to stay afloat by paying their bills, and later by supporting the recovery. This funding didn't last for more than a few months.

By contrast, large-scale borrowing to fund public projects and create good-paying jobs for everyone was tried during the 1960s and 1970s—not just for a few months, but for decades. It ultimately failed, as persistent inflation punished everyone.

Risk of crowding-out effect from public deficits

Another consequence of the public deficit happens within the financial markets. To cover its deficit, the government monopolizes the cheapest lending, taking it away from the private sector. This phenomenon is referred to as the so-called "***crowding-out effect***," which is characterized by numerous borrowers competing for cheap loans. Ineluctably, interest rates have to rise when affordable lending options become depleted.

This crowding-out adversely affects corporations. Their profits are squeezed by higher interest expenses and by the loss of income from secondary investments that become unprofitable under elevated rates. With reduced corporate output, the crowding-out effect tends to increase inflationary pressures, even though higher interest rates also reduce consumer spending.

The resulting inflationary tensions force the Fed to raise interest rates to contain the price rise, in order to comply with its current mandate. Since the 1980s, the annoyance of the 1970-style inflation has been de-facto replaced by the grinding of high interest rates induced by the Fed, which can add up on top of the crowding-out effect on interest rates resulting from the deep public deficit.

If the government runs a persistent deficit to "save the world," the Fed would have to stay the course, keeping politically neutral and raising interest rates. That path would almost certainly bring higher unemployment and an economic slump, caused by crippling interest rates caused by the government's expansive borrowing. This downturn would come even if inflation stayed under control.

Nowadays, the economic consensus holds that excessive government intervention and large public deficits, financed through taxation and borrowing, can drain resources from corporations and stifle entrepreneurial spirit as well as the individual initiative of workers. Nimble capitalist enterprises, motivated by the need to enhance efficiency and reduce costs, is the only effective path to bolster the Treasury's revenue through taxation.

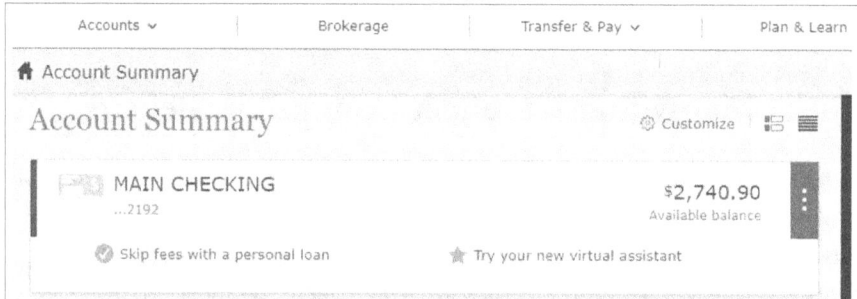

The money sitting in deposit accounts is not pilling in the bank's vault. While the bank owes the account holder the deposited funds, it does not keep all that money on hand. Most of it is typically invested in corporate or Treasury bonds or lent out to other customers. In the end, only a small fraction of the money in checking or savings accounts is held in the bank's vault to accommodate customer cash withdrawal requests.

Any additional sale of Treasury bonds cannot rely on money that banks do not physically hold; it can only draw on existing cash reserves held by private investors. As a result, Treasury bonds must offer competitive interest rates to attract that capital, which may, in turn, reduce the funds available for other corporate investments.

The money illusion

It is imperative to reiterate that irresponsible borrowing is only blessed by fools suffering from "*money illusion*" when they view wealth and income in nominal money value, without taking into account the real value adjusted for inflation.

Worse, fully-fledged demagogy of a misguided government borrowing endlessly from its central bank could fuel hyperinflation.

This is particularly dramatic in countries such as in Germany in the 1920s, Argentina in the 1970s or Zimbabwe in the late 2000s.

This money illusion can be attributed to inadequate financial education among the public, the media, and even intellectuals who are easily dazzled by stacks of banknotes as a panacea. This illusion fosters the rise of populists who promise unlimited borrowing as a solution to global problems. The spread of such monetary misconceptions is extremely dangerous and can have far-reaching consequences.

In reality, the government can't compel banks to pay with the money that they don't have, in order to provide well-paid jobs that don't exist yet. The weekly wages would be spent way before any slow output, which would pressure prices upward and hit the economy with inflation. Dangerous inflationary pressure from money shoveled to the masses can severely disrupt the economy. These tactics certainly won't provide food for all, green tech for a carbon-free world and military protection for allies. This inept solution would only level down society at the poorest bottom.

Prior to considering reckless private or public borrowing, one must understand that money is like a number, a counter or a fuel gauge (as in the picture). In this sense, people must effectively fill the tank before they can drive as long as the fuel gauge indicates that there is gasoline in the tank.

Excessive borrowing to allow the distribution of free dollars is like tampering with the gauge to indicate a full tank without producing gasoline and refilling the car. Despite the gauge indicating a full tank, the car won't go as far as expected. The amount of gasoline is determined by the many hours of numerous hardworking people in oil wells all the way to replenishing gas stations, not by manipulating the fuel gauge with a populist decree.

No, Overtaxing High Incomes Is Not a Panacea

Jacking up taxes on high wages and corporate profits?

Some propose a straightforward solution for the government to fund projects targeting social inequalities: increasing tax rates on affluent individuals and their corporations. This argument advocates for government intervention to levy higher taxes on these entities, with the aim of funding infrastructure, expanding healthcare facilities, and creating well-paid jobs. This approach is viewed as a counterbalance to the private sector's inadequacies in addressing low wages.

After all, higher tax rates were prevalent during the post-war period and the economy was humming with higher wages. Shouldn't the people unite to impose a fair taxation system to finance a full-employment economy with lower inequalities? Isn't it a no-brainer to demand a tax rate increase, which is blocked by the greedy rich hoarding their cash and conspiring with their lobbyists in Washington?

Robin Hood for President? Just raise all tax rates on the rich and on their corporations, then the government can spend, create jobs, and solve it all?

Yes, Robin Hood could have helped his people by stealing the coins hoarded by the greedy Rich. In the medieval period, the circulation of precious coins was crucial for economic transactions, but there was a shortage of gold and silver for coinage due to the scarcity of mines.

Today, dollars deposited in savings accounts are not idle; they generate additional dollars through loans and investments in production, which must precede consumption. Therefore, high tax rates can deplete funds intended for new ventures, and a dollar taxed from the wealthy does not necessarily translate into jobs or affordable goods for the poor.

It is essential to recognize that advancements such as longer life expectancy and lower child mortality, have resulted from private investments in producing essential goods like soap and water pipes. Redirecting funds from investments in competitive corporations to inefficient government-run public projects risks outcomes similar to those of communist regimes in Russia and China during the 20th century.

Heavy taxation: A political threat

A first principle of taxation is the necessity of moderation. Individuals must retain sufficient private resources to own independent media outlets, hire lawyers or bodyguards, and enjoy the leisure needed to express themselves. This right, which safeguards against potential government overreach, is an essential component of historical charters aimed at curbing despotism, such as the Magna Carta (1215), the US Constitution (1787), and the Universal Declaration of Human Rights (1948), further reinforced by the International Covenant on Civil and Political Rights (1966).

With abusive taxation, an authoritarian faction—even if representing the majority—could silence dissent. Nothing is easier than forcing political opponents into the harsh labor of subsistence. Election rigging is then legitimized by state-controlled media muzzled by the ruling council. Finally, an ambitious dictator is free to eliminate rivals through sham lawsuits or orchestrated accidents.

In this sense, abusive taxation—even in the name of helping the poor—is both pernicious and specious. History has repeatedly shown that regimes replacing private initiative with state bureaucracies have failed economically, impoverished many, and too often descended into totalitarianism.

Better a communist govern-ment closely monitored by the people united, instead of omnipotent private corpora-tions responsible for low wages, inequality, even pollu-tion?

Warning: past experiments have shown many risks associ-ated with communist regimes. Communism has a poor record for improving people's lives, let alone of protecting the environment. Soviet wealth was all in the hands of the communist elite, not the people. China isn't much more equal, only surmounting extreme poverty by allowing capitalism around Shenzhen or Shanghai.

In front of the poor results, benevolent politicians tend to be overthrown by ruthless challengers in order to "save" the regime (e.g., as these two in the picture who jailed their rivals). These dictators prioritize maintaining their grip on power over addressing issues like curbing inequalities or global warming. They are more likely to hide the true figures of poverty or GHG emissions, suppress free press, and quell public dissent.

High taxes and the stagflation of the 1970s

High tax rates on incomes were already tried in the past, notably during the 1950s. During this period, the marginal income tax rate reached 91% under the US federal income tax, and the corporate tax rate exceeded 50%. This resulted in an effective tax rate of approxi-mately 42% for the wealthiest taxpayers, who could compensate them-selves with stocks or dividends, optimizing for lower tax rates and potential deductions. These tax rates were among the highest in histor-ical records.

This strategy began to backfire in the late 1960s and 1970s, a period marked by increased government spending driven by factors such as the Vietnam War, the Apollo space program, and President Johnson's "Great Society" welfare programs. The adverse long-term economic consequences of inflated tax rates became evident during this time. The high tax rates proved counterproductive for several underlying reasons:

- Business relocation: People move their business to countries with more favorable tax environments or engage in legal tax-exempt schemes, effectively reducing the domestic tax base.

- Shift to the Underground Economy: People conceal their business in the underground economy, perhaps receiving unemployment checks while working in the underground economy.

- Reduced Consumer Spending: Taxation lowers workers' disposable income, limiting spending mainly to everyday staples and potentially reducing corporate output and employment in more sophisticated goods and services.

- Investment Impediment: Punishing taxation reduces the capital available to both wealthy and middle-class individuals for investment in new ventures. Such investments are crucial for job creation and for providing goods and services to the people.

High taxes, therefore, can impede work, consumption, investment, and innovation by diverting funds away from the productive purposes that fuel economic growth. This reduction in the production of goods and services contributed to inflation, as the ratio of money over goods increases. Attempts by the government to stimulate the economy through escalating deficit spending further exacerbated inflation, as discussed in the previous chapter. This situation culminated in a scenario where, as economists often describe, an excess of money was chasing a limited supply of goods, intensifying a vicious circle of inflationary pressures and economic slowdown.

The 1970s marked the culmination of a period known as "*stagflation*," characterized by economic stagnation coupled with inflation. This era reached a critical point when unemployment levels escalated to what was termed "mass unemployment." These economic challenges served as a valuable lesson for policy makers. There is now a broad recognition that excessive taxation proved ineffective in this past experiment. Many experts agree that this approach is unlikely to yield positive results in the future and poses a risk to the principles of democracy.

Contrary to popular belief, the government does not itself perform miracles such as building roads or feeding the poor. Instead, its role is largely fiscal: it collects funds from individuals and corporations and channels those resources to the private sector to carry out projects and services. For example, the construction of roads, dams, and military equipment is typically outsourced to private corporations through a public bidding process, which fosters competition. Similarly, in welfare programs, the government rarely provides goods or services directly. Instead, recipients of programs like food stamps or Medicare use their handouts to purchase what they need from private providers, retaining the freedom to choose their suppliers.

The government's involvement in the management of public services is concentrated in sectors where the presence of private corporations might not align with the public's best interest. Only then, the government establishes monopolistic entities, which are operated by civil servants. These entities function within a framework where operational guidelines, pricing structures, and regulatory standards are determined by the bureaucratic processes of local, state, or federal legislative bodies. Notable examples of such government-operated sectors include K-12 education, the armed forces, police departments, and public utilities.

In the end, the government relies on the private sector to provide products and services to the public. This practice is considered more efficient compared to historical instances of extensive governmental control, such as those observed in the USSR and during the regulatory excesses of the 1970s.

Since 1980, cutting tax rates for more(!) fiscal revenues

The stagflation and mass unemployment of the 1970s catalyzed a shift in tax policy and economic thought. This economic failure paved the way for the acceptance of an alternative economic perspective.

By around 1980, new economic theories emerged to challenge the 1970s-style taxation of the wealthy. They argued that such high taxation inadvertently harmed the most vulnerable by depriving them of work. The resulting reduction in private investment—siphoned away by the IRS—hindered the creation of new enterprises and slowed economic growth. Over time, this dynamic could also reduce tax revenues, limiting the government's ability to effectively fund essential services such as education and welfare.

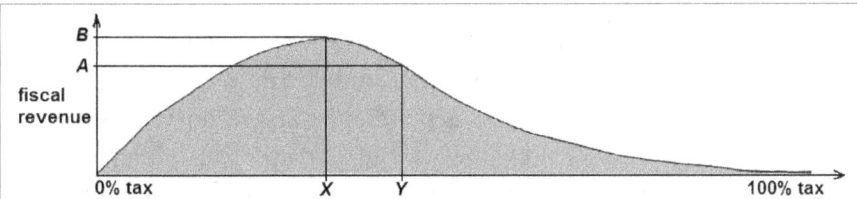

*Higher tax rates can bring less income to the government, not more! The economist Arthur Laffer illustrated it with his "**Laffer curve**":*

• On the left, at 0% tax rate, tax revenue is obviously zero. As the tax rate increases from this point, government revenue also begins to rise—a seemingly straightforward correlation.

• On the right, at a 100% tax rate, no one works intensely—except for Stakhanovites or model workers—since all wages are collected and redistributed by distant bureaucracies, with no regard for individual productivity. As a result, production falls to Stalinist levels as workers lose motivation and investors withdraw. At the same time, tax revenues collapse.

• To join both ends of the curve, the rising tendency on the left has to curb beyond a certain point. It happens when taxation becomes excessive, discouraging work, deterring investments, and fueling the underground economy. The curve is then flattening before decreasing with taxes starved by plunging profits and discouraging post-tax wages.

According to this curve, any tax percentage higher than the top of the curve (X) means that a tax cut—instead of a rate hike(!)—is counter-intuitively required to increase tax incomes! Yet, lowering the tax rate from Y to X will increase fiscal revenues from A to B only after a few years, because it takes time for investments and work motivation to come back. In the short term, a tax rate hike will bring more immediate revenue to the government.

Since the 1980s, the implementation of tax cuts has helped the economy recover from recurrent downturns. Despite ongoing challenges like persistent unemployment and wage stagnation in certain sectors, these fiscal policy adjustments have played a key role in revitalizing the economy.

Cutting tax rates to stem the economic crisis

To overcome the economic crisis of the 1970s, President Reagan signed laws to cut federal income taxation from a maximum tax rate of 70% to 50% with the Economic Recovery Tax Act of 1981, and then cut it down to 28% with the Tax Reform Act of 1986. Subsequent years saw fluctuations in the maximum tax rate from the 1990s to the 2020s, influenced by the prevailing majority in Congress. Despite these changes, the tax rates have not reverted to the peak levels experienced in the 1970s.

The primary objective of the tax cuts was to stimulate private investment. By increasing net income, individuals were encouraged to invest in financial markets, such as purchasing stocks on Wall Street, or to allocate funds into local businesses and startups. This policy enabled not only the wealthy but also the middle class to invest the additional income retained after taxation.

Furthermore, the tax cuts were anticipated to boost consumer spending, particularly among the lower income groups, who tend to have a higher propensity to spend. This contrasted with the upper classes, who generally maintained consistent consumption levels. Illustrative of this approach, the lowest bracket of the federal tax rate was reduced from 14% to 11% in 1981, a move specifically targeted to increase disposable income and stimulate spending among those in the lower income brackets.

After 1982, the economy started to recover. It was the rise of "supply-side economics," with its emphasis on the production of goods, moving away from the constraints of high tax rates, ineffective regulations, and prevailing inflation. In this climate, corporations found it easier to secure financing, employ workers, and market their products to the middle class. The strategy relied on the middle class being able to make purchases with their incomes, thus circumventing the challenges of unemployment and inflation prevalent in the 1970s. Despite the crises of 1991, 2001, and 2008, this supply-side approach has continued to dominate economic policy.

Cutting tax rates on capital gains for a new economy

Another response to the economic challenges of the 1970s was a series of successive reductions in capital gains tax rates under the administrations of Presidents Carter, Reagan, and Clinton. These tax cuts, implemented in 1978, 1981, and 1997, proved economically beneficial, particularly evident in the growth of the 1980s and 1990s. They stimulated investments in startups, facilitated through venture capital and

Initial Public Offerings ("*IPOs*") in stock markets such as the NYSE and NASDAQ.

The lower tax rates of the 1980s and 1990s were instrumental in transitioning the economy away from traditional industries, paving the way for the emergence of a new economic landscape in the US. This shift not only revitalized the domestic economy but also had an impact internationally, with the European Union, among others, benefiting from the resultant boost in productivity and economic growth. These developments underscore the far-reaching implications of tax policies on the economy.

The recovery has not lifted low wages

After 1982, the economy halted its decline and began recovering in most sectors. However, this period has been marked by a persistent stagnation in middle-class wages. The situation is more pronounced for low-income earners, whose wages have actually decreased when adjusted for inflation. This decline can be attributed to factors such as the increased use of robotics, the influx of cheaper imports, and the relocation of manufacturing to foreign countries. Only the highest wages, particularly of those involved in high-tech products, have increased over these decades.

Economists are puzzled by this wage stagnation, especially when compared to the wage growth observed in previous periods of economic recovery. They can't explain how a tightening unemployment hasn't led to a wage increase. They can only confess lacking data to investigate the root causes among the potential culprits.

There is also growing concern among some economists that the tax cuts may have inadvertently contributed to the rise of a new high-tech economy that displaces workers and exerts downward pressure on low-skill wages. The rise of artificial intelligence and self-driving vehicles could potentially perpetuate the stagnation of low-skill wages indefinitely.

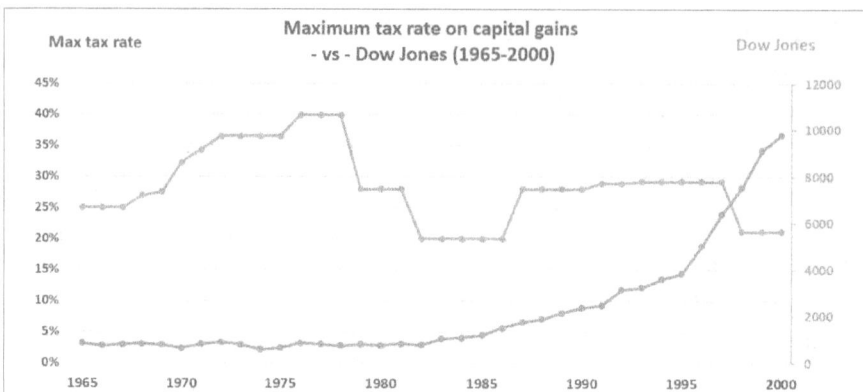

Lower tax rates allow venture capitalists and middle-class wage earners to retain more of their income. Much of this money is invested or reinvested into startups or stock market IPOs, though a portion may be spent on luxury goods. Such funding is vital for tech ventures, since banks are often reluctant to lend to young entrepreneurs with revolutionary ideas. Likewise, governments hesitate to back high-risk startups because their high failure rates—around 90%—could trigger political backlash.

The surge of the stock market, fueled by these dynamics, has attracted increased investment and a higher number of IPOs, thereby financing the burgeoning tech economy, with startups growing into tech giants, such as Genentech, Google or Amazon. This growth has also indirectly benefited the US Treasury, as evidenced by increased tax revenues from capital gains following each of the tax cuts in 1978, 1981, and 1997.

The downside was that the expansion of the stock market increased the wealth of the richest individuals, creating a disparity in wealth distribution. Concurrently, although unemployment rates decreased, there was a notable absence of wage growth for low-income workers. This growing economic inequality has become a source of dissatisfaction across the nation.

A comeback of high tax rates won't fix inequality

Ignoring the failures of the past, a radical government might choose to sharply raise all tax rates. Such a high-tax strategy would reduce the earnings of the wealthy, but it would not create large numbers of jobs under government direction. Any increase in tax revenue would be short-lived, since it would never match the productive investments that might have been made with the confiscated money. Instead, it would produce politicized spending rather than sound investments—a pattern that has often fueled inflation, damaging the economy and long-term tax revenues. At best, it could recreate the stagflation of the 1970s; at worst, it could resemble the stagnation of the Soviet Union.

Such a high-tax strategy would disproportionately hurt the poor by slowing the economy and increasing unemployment. It would achieve the opposite of its intended effect. It would only deepen inequality between political elites and the masses of the poor. History shows that taxation alone cannot solve social problems; more often, it produces greater poverty and political instability.

To reduce poverty, it is better to cap tax rates at today's moderate levels. Ideally, this approach will remain the norm. Variations in these rates should stay small—perhaps rising slightly when Congress leans left or falling modestly when the right holds sway. Overall, these limited fluctuations within capped rates can be expected to provide the Treasury with a stable stream of revenue.

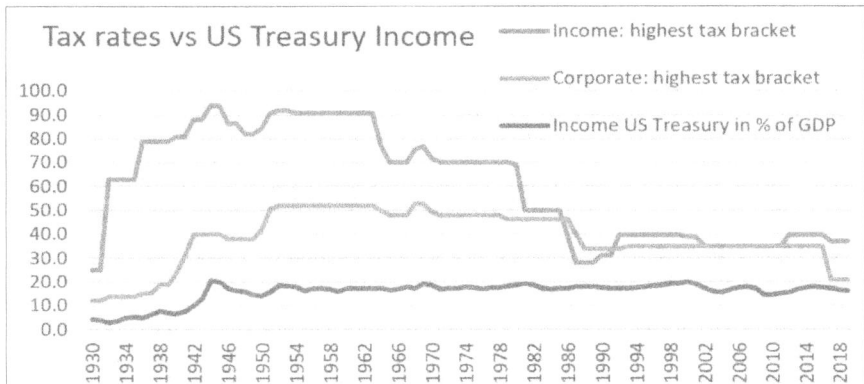

*High tax rates never made the US Treasury much richer in the past. The "**effective tax rate**"—the actual percentage of income paid by individuals and corporations—has not been much higher than it is today, averaging around 20% of GDP. It is therefore inaccurate to suggest that the postwar economic expansion occurred despite high tax rates, or that the lower tax rates of the 1980s reduced federal revenue.*

The relatively low tax collections of the 1950s and 1960s may have been partly due to tax avoidance and the use of exemptions. However, there should be no rush to eliminate all deductions and exemptions, treating them merely as loopholes. Many tax breaks play a critical role in encouraging risk-taking and innovation. Such incentives can enhance skills and expertise across fields from healthcare to defense, create jobs, and ultimately increase future tax revenues. Raising tax rates without preserving deductions could be counterproductive. Such measures risk job losses and widespread impoverishment by shifting focus from productive private enterprise to bureaucratic management. Industry leaders could be replaced by less efficient government appointees, hindering economic growth and innovation—ultimately harming everyone.

No, a Wealth Tax Won't Fund Good Wages for All

Congress should just pass a new wealth tax, right?

There is a prevalent view that the very rich could reasonably be subject to increased taxation. Advocates of this approach argue that Congress should implement a new wealth tax, when income tax rates can't go much higher as learned since the 1970s. The argument behind this proposition is that it would empower the government to create well-paid jobs and fund solutions to all the problems of the world. Following this perspective, Congress must impose a wealth tax to address the situation.

Oxfam 2024: "billionaires are $3.3 trillion richer than they were in 2020"

Many sensational newspaper headlines imply that the wealthy earn trillions and that solving the world's problems is straightforward. In reality, most of this wealth is not liquid cash but is tied up in corporate shares valued according to the latest Wall Street quotations. Converting such wealth into cash on a large scale is highly impractical. If the wealthy were forced to sell large numbers of shares to pay a punitive tax, the lack of suffi-cient buyers could trigger a collapse in share prices. This situation would resemble a game of musical chairs, with wealthy individuals unable to hold all the shares and only low-income individuals to purchase them with their limited savings. Such a collapse would make it impossible to raise the necessary funds to pay the taxes on wealth. In the worst-case scenario, these punitive measures against the wealthy could echo the Russian deku-lakization of the post-1917 era, which led to widespread economic and social upheaval.

The cash of the rich is gone—tied up in loans or investments

A major misconception is the belief that the super-rich sit on piles of cash. In reality, their cash is largely gone, tied up in investments that contribute to economic growth. Much of this wealth has been allocated to acquiring corporate shares that yield dividends or government bonds that pay interest. Their investments also extend to real estate, building housing complexes and generating rental income. Some funds may also have been used to purchase assets such as gold ingots, seen as a hedge against currency devaluation. Only a small amount of cash remains in checking accounts, and even this typically circulates through the banking system, where deposits are used by banks to purchase bonds or extend loans.

Altogether, the assets of the wealthy are typically in the form of debt instruments, rather than hard cash. This composition makes it challenging to tax this wealth for funding infrastructure projects, educational initiatives, or even green energy ventures. To pay a substantial wealth tax, these assets would need to be converted into cash before the tax deadline. This process, involving the large-scale liquidation of debt instruments, is not straightforward, far from it.

A wealth tax could still be applied to the remaining cash assets stored in investment and banking accounts. However, it is important to consider that this cash has already been taxed, either through income tax or capital gains tax. Furthermore, cash held in investment or banking accounts is often already loaned out through the bond market, money markets, Certificates of Deposit, or other financial instruments.

Is it the greedy rich (as guilty as in Bruegel's painting of the seven deadly sins) who are lobbying politicians to reject a wealth tax, which could fund job creation with good wages and solve it all?

No, not quite. The proposition that plundering the rich's wealth valued in billions of dollars would single-handedly resolve all societal issues is overly simplistic and does not fully grasp the true nature of economic realities.

The delusion lies in equating one dollar in wealth with one dollar in liquid cash or with one dollar in tangible output like bread. In reality, the cash was long ago invested in assets like machinery in exchange for a debt instrument. This resulting debt-title valued in dollars is not equal to the dollars' worth of bread in practical terms. They are valued the same in monetary units, but they are not interchangeable. The dollar serves merely as a unit of measurement for value, not value itself. To increase output, such as bread production, the focus should be on expanding arable land and improving crop yields, rather than attempting to extract value from non-liquid assets like machinery.

The conversion of assets such as debt instruments, or machinery into liquid cash necessitates their sale in the market. This process can be undertaken at will but is not feasible for rapid, large-scale liquidation, especially under the constraint of a wealth tax. The scenario where wealthy individuals are compelled to sell their assets, all valued in dollars, is impractical, as the rich cannot be a seller and buyer at the same time to accumulate cash for tax obligations. Moreover, the poor cannot participate as buyers due to their limited cash savings.

The misconception about the nature of wealth is prevalent among journalists and politicians. Wealth, which can be measured by aggregating the dollar value of various assets, must not be mistaken for liquid cash or essential commodities like food. The process of converting these assets into cash or necessary goods is neither direct nor immediate. Misinterpreting these disparate financial figures can confuse the public and does little to advance practical solutions to fundamental needs. This understanding is essential for accurately assessing economic resources and their potential impact on society.

Non-cash assets are difficult to tax

A wealth tax would require taxpayers to self-report their wealth until the administration develops a system for verifying the assets of millions of citizens.

The valuation of these assets should align with their current market value. For publicly traded stocks, a standard valuation method, such as the "200-day moving average" could be used, acknowledging the inherent volatility in stock market valuations. For privately held stocks, the valuation could be based on the dividends distributed over recent years. A similar approach, focusing on yield, would be applicable for the assessment of other types of assets, ensuring a consistent and fair evaluation methodology.

Not too fast, then! Implementing a 2% wealth tax could have significant economic implications. Such taxation could reduce risk-taking among investors, as the inability to offset losses with after-tax gains may discourage investment in future growth. Over time, this could harm the broader economy and even reduce government tax revenues, as suggested by the principles of the Laffer Curve.

A high wealth tax is unrealistic

A careful analysis is required when considering the implementation of a high wealth tax, such as the annual rate of over 3–4% proposed by some policymakers. Taxpayers would not be able to cover such a tax solely from dividends, since the average after-tax yield on stock dividends is typically only 1–2% of the stock's value in an average year. These taxpayers would need to sell portions of their stocks or bonds to meet their tax obligations. This raises the question of who would buy those assets.

Other wealthy individuals would not be likely buyers, since they too would be under pressure to sell assets to meet the same tax requirements. The wealthy cannot all buy and sell simultaneously to raise cash for taxes—it simply does not make sense. Nor could they realistically borrow funds to pay the tax, as banks would hesitate to issue such loans knowing that borrowers would struggle to find buyers with sufficient cash to purchase the assets.

The middle class is unlikely to fill this gap, since the average household has limited cash reserves. Most people's liquid assets, such as savings, are far smaller than their non-liquid assets, like the value of their homes.

In this scenario, there is a real risk of a downward spiral in stock prices due to a shortage of buyers. Because the majority of the stock market is owned by the affluent, a collective rush to sell could trigger a market crash. Even the super-rich might struggle to sell assets at reasonable prices to raise the cash needed to pay the tax. In extreme cases, this could prompt wealthy individuals to relocate to countries without a wealth tax to avoid bankruptcy in the United States.

Cash constitutes only a small portion of total assets. According to Federal Reserve data, the total cash supply, represented by the monetary aggregate M2, was approximately 15 trillion dollars in 2019. In comparison, the total asset valuation on Wall Street was about 30 trillion dollars as of 2018, as reported by the World Bank. This figure does not even include the stocks of corporations not listed on Wall Street, Treasury bonds, or gold ingots.

Given that the top 1% of wealth holders own a significant portion of Wall Street's stocks and bonds, imposing a 5% wealth tax on them would necessitate mobilizing a considerable amount of cash, possibly amounting to trillions of dollars, for the repurchase of these assets. Such a large-scale mobilization of cash could result in reduced cash availability for the general population to purchase goods and services, potentially impacting the overall economy.

Therefore, the idea of taxing non-cash assets (which are valued in dollars but are not actual cash) and distributing the proceeds as free cash to the people fails to account for the practical challenges associated with liquidating non-cash assets and the potential economic repercussions of such actions.

Asset confiscation will not revive the economy

Instead of direct cash payments to satisfy a high wealth tax, an alternative approach could involve the government confiscating a certain percentage of stocks, such as 1 out of every 10 shares. This strategy would avoid the need for problematic cash payments from the wealthy to the Treasury, thereby circumventing issues related to insufficient market liquidity to purchase the shares.

This system would, over time, nationalize corporations as the government accumulated shares through years of stock-based tax payments. The result would be a bureaucratic command economy, with corporations increasingly managed by government officials, whose decisions are influenced more by union pressures and social demands than by market competition and customer needs. Historically, governments have shown a poor track record in corporate management. Such centralized control could reduce profitability, hinder reinvestment in productive assets, and ultimately diminish economic output. The consequences might include lower sales, fewer jobs, a general decline in economic well-being, and an increasingly authoritarian, state-directed economy.

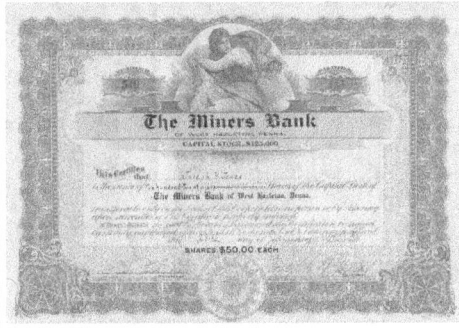

The rich don't sit on a pile of cash, but on a pile of financial securities—such as shares and debt instruments (as in the picture). In other words, the rich "only" own the means of production, not the output, which is mostly consumed by the people. And, the people want the output, not necessarily owning the means of production. The former may be owned by a few, but only the latter can be consumed by everyone through purchase in dollars. And no, the former can't be converted into the latter with a magic wand, even if they are both valued in dollars. It results that the government can never tax the rich from the cash that they don't have and spend it to solve all the problems of the world.

*The rich don't earn large amounts of cash year after year; rather, they see the market value of their assets rise. This misunderstanding can be seen as an advanced form of the money illusion, evolving into what can be termed a "**money delusion**," where wealth is inaccurately perceived as readily available cash. This view disregards the complexities involved in converting non-liquid assets to cash. Such oversimplifications create a distorted view of wealth, leading to impractical taxation policies, which scrape together only small amounts of cash for short-term, demagogic spending—at the dangerous expense of long-term investment. This money delusion is akin to the medieval perception of wealth as gold or silver coins, when such coins were scarce. Those who hold this view obsessively believe that confiscating imaginary hoards of gold and silver can resolve all the world's problems.*

Furthermore, individuals affected by the money illusion often believe that simply throwing money at a problem will solve it. These advocates have pushed for generous welfare programs since President Johnson's Great Society, yet such programs have not resolved the underlying issues. Many even argue that they backfired—fostering idleness, boredom, drug abuse, and crime. Effective solutions require more than just financial resources; they demand personal responsibility and sustained hard work.

Switzerland: Wealth tax success in a low-tax country

Switzerland shows that a wealth tax can be implemented effectively, as evidenced by its long-standing system. The tax is levied at a rate of less than 1% annually, striking a balance between revenue generation and maintaining a moderate burden. While Switzerland does impose a wealth tax, it is important to note that the country's overall tax burden —its **"tax-to-GDP ratio"** measured by international agencies—is comparable to that of the US and relatively low compared with typical EU standards.

In the EU, several countries, including France, have discontinued the wealth tax due to its unintended consequences. The implementation of the wealth tax in these regions resulted in the expatriation of wealth, which did not contribute to the domestic economy as intended. Historical precedents, such as those observed in the 1970s and in various EU countries, demonstrate that excessive taxation of income or wealth can have counterproductive effects. Currently, the EU is experiencing a shortfall in private capital. This deficiency is hindering the region's ability to emulate the successful model of the US in several key areas. These include the development of innovative technologies, the nurturing of emerging startups, and the investment in vital sectors such as Artificial Intelligence, military advancements, or even green technology.

In the US, a form of wealth taxation is already in place through the property tax levied on real estate. The US also imposes a capital gains tax, which would overlap with a concurrent wealth tax, as explained below. In contrast, Switzerland does not impose a capital gains tax on stock investments, opting only for a wealth tax.

Alternative tax on wealth: The capital gains tax

In the US, the capital gains tax exists to rein in the infinite increase in asset valuations, primarily benefiting the wealthiest individuals. This tax is imposed on the profit realized from the sale of assets, which is determined by comparing the sale price with the original purchase price. The application of capital gains tax at the exact moment of asset sale ensures a clear and unambiguous determination of the taxable amount, offering a more straightforward approach compared to the complex nature of a wealth tax.

Effective from 2020, the US federal tax regime imposes a 37% capital gains tax on short-term investments, categorized as assets held for a duration of less than one year. This federal rate is further augmented by state-level taxes, with California imposing taxes as high as 13.3%. However, this short-term rate is infrequently paid by wealthy individuals. This is because such individuals commonly engage in short-term trading through hedge funds based in tax havens. These hedge funds are not subject to taxation, provided the assets are continuously traded and remain within the funds.

As of 2024, the federal tax rate on long-term holdings has been reduced to 20%. There are several reasons put forward to justify this lower rate. First, the earnings of shareholders have already been subjected to corporate taxes. Second, the tax structure needs to take into account the potential losses investors face due to the high failure rates of startups. Third, studies suggest that raising capital gains tax rates tends to reduce IRS revenues. This reduction is attributed to the tendency of individuals to avoid taxation by keeping their assets, possibly within foreign hedge funds, while resorting to borrowing against these holdings for personal expenditures until a future reduction in tax rates. Finally, taxing capital gain tends to produce cyclical revenue that fluctuates with Wall Street's business cycles. This volatility makes it challenging to reliably forecast public spending.

The tax rates currently in place are the focus of extensive debates, which fall beyond the scope of this book. Nonetheless, it is noteworthy to mention that these forms of taxation present a more feasible approach to asset taxation when compared to the challenges associated with implementing a wealth tax.

Taxing unrealized capital gains has been proposed as a measure aimed at high-net-worth individuals who rarely sell their stocks and therefore pay little in capital gains. Only a few thousand wealthy individuals would be targeted by this proposal. They would sell some shares to obtain the cash to pay the tax, but not enough to trigger the kind of unrealistic hot-potato dynamic described with a wealth tax.

The opponents of such taxation blocked it in Congress for reasons similar to the rejection of a wealth tax. They insist that such a tax would be counterproductive:

• *Redirection of Investment Funds:* Opponents argue that this tax would divert money away from private investments, which they contend are usually managed more efficiently than government projects. If those funds shift to government control, the economy could slow down—and in the long run, tax revenue might even shrink instead of increase.

• *Disproportionate Impact on Successful Entrepreneurs:* The structure of this tax places a burden on highly successful business owners. As the value of their assets increases, so does their tax liability. This could force prominent entrepreneurs, like Elon Musk, to scale back on innovative projects, and philanthropists, like Bill Gates, to curtail their charitable activities, in favor of meeting tax obligations—a scenario perceived as favoring bureaucracy.

• *Competitive Disadvantage for Domestic Investors:* Finally, critics argue that such a tax is un-American in spirit, as it would place American investors at a relative disadvantage compared to foreign investors who would be exempt from this tax.

The inescapable tax on wealth: The estate tax

An alternative method for taxing wealth is through estate and gift taxes, which levy taxes at the point of inheritance. Beneficiaries can opt to liquidate assets and pay the tax due through an installment plan spanning ten years, a provision permitted by the IRS. This strategy offers a more manageable payment system compared to a recurring wealth tax. It is important to note that the estate tax is closely linked with the gift tax. This linkage is designed to prevent individuals from circumventing the estate tax by transferring their wealth as gifts during their lifetime.

In the US, the federal law imposes a tax of up to 40% on inheritances or gifts exceeding $14 million. Additionally, 13 states levy their own estate tax. This $14 million federal exemption doesn't dent the collection of the estate tax on the super-rich, as their fortunes often measure in the billions, making this exemption a negligible portion of their total wealth.

The exemption is designed to protect small businesses, such as corporations and farms, facilitating their retention within the same family across generations. It serves as an incentive for small business owners, encouraging them to pursue long-term investments. It assures them that they can bequeath their entire business to their heirs without the encumbrance of estate tax. This promotes the continuity and stability of family-owned enterprises.

An alternative approach to taxing the wealthy could involve implementing taxes on luxury consumption. This method targets conspicuous expenditure rather than imposing a general wealth tax, which could potentially hinder investment, slow economic growth, and adversely affect low-income workers.

This concept was put into practice in the US in 1991, with the introduction of a 10% surcharge tax on high-end items such as yachts, private jets, jewelry, and other luxury goods. However, this tax was short-lived; just two years after its implementation, it was repealed following lobbying efforts, particularly from the luxury yacht industry, which pointed to job losses as a consequence of the tax.

In a free-market economy, not all forms of taxation can be effectively integrated. It is crucial to establish a fiscal equilibrium that stimulates economic growth and job creation while optimizing long-term tax revenue.

No miracle in plundering the rich

The idea that taxing the wealthy alone can solve low wages and inequality is a misconception. This stems from the fact that the affluent do not consume all the goods themselves; rather, they own the means of production, such as machinery and corporations. These assets are not readily convertible into liquid cash instantaneously; they represent long-term investments and are integral to the production process.

Therefore, expecting immediate financial gains from their liquidation just doesn't make any sense.

This reality does not exclude the possibility of a wealth tax. A measured approach to wealth taxation, akin to the model implemented in Switzerland, can be justified to curb the potential for undue political influence by the ultra-wealthy. However, implementing such a tax might necessitate adjustments to the current tax framework, which could include reconsidering or eliminating the capital gains tax.

On the other hand, a gigantic wealth tax will never fund the extensive creation of well-paying jobs through large-scale public works for building hospitals, roads, schools, or a green transition to fix climate change.

The only sea change that could be enacted is a confiscation of wealth, such as outright expropriation in a manner akin to historical communist regimes, or an annual 10% wealth tax leading to complete nationalization over a decade. This approach didn't revitalize the USSR or Maoist China. In many instances, it only transferred the wealth from private individuals to totalitarian masters.

The belief that the rich are only rich at the expense of the poor is simplistic. If this were the case, communist-style redistribution would have resolved such inequities. On the contrary, communist administrations of the past have significantly under-performed the free market of industrial minds and venture capitalists. Monopolistic management by apparatchiks may have kept prices low, but with long lines at the shops.

No, the Government Can't Make Corporations Hire and Pay More

Should the government guide corporations toward better pay and jobs?

There is a growing call for stricter regulations on corporations, particularly measures mandating comprehensive wage increases and job creation. This movement stems from the observation that many of these companies boast multi-trillion-dollar valuations and generate substantial profits. Given this financial capacity, some argue that they have a responsibility to provide better wages for their low-income employees.

Several public policy initiatives could be considered to increase job opportunities and improve wage conditions for low-income workers. These initiatives might include raising the minimum wage, establishing hiring quotas, or mandating union membership to give workers greater bargaining power in wage negotiations.

Supporters contend that such higher wages could stimulate consumer spending and strengthen the broader economy. Research suggests that even a modest rise in wages can increase overall spending, drive GDP growth, and support higher employment levels.

The legacy of postwar incremental guidance: A controversial approach

Proponents of such gradually tightened regulations claim that this strategy was successful during the postwar boom in steering corporations toward growth. The approach was shaped by the belief that the private sector was incapable of recovering on its own and providing jobs for all, as seen in the aftermath of the 1929 crisis.

The focus was on demand as the primary driver of the economy. The demand-side economists challenged the notion of tax reductions for the affluent. Instead, they championed increased government expenditure as a means to stimulate economic growth by creating additional employment opportunities. Their justification was that if consumer spending declined and businesses were hesitant to hire and invest in new facilities, the government had to step in.

By raising minimum wages and applying hiring pressures, the government could stimulate demand for goods and services. It could also use incentives such as tax breaks, or impose penalties, to encourage companies to hire unemployed youth and individuals facing long-term joblessness.

The postwar governments were confident about their ability to guide the economy toward a virtuous cycle of enhanced demand, robust growth, and full employment. This regulatory approach appeared effective in the post-war period. The US industry nimbly transitioned from wartime to post-war production to cater to the surging peacetime demands.

Opponents of such historical analysis argue that it worked during the postwar period only because economic growth was the true driver of rising wages and a healthy job market. Corporations sought to expand their market share and could adapt to any government guidance.

Mandating higher pay can backfire

Many economists are skeptical that gradually raising the minimum wage will stimulate economic growth. They argue that corporations may simply stop hiring if wages are pushed above the value of the work performed. While some workers may benefit from higher pay, less productive workers may lose their jobs or never be hired—creating a vicious cycle of higher unemployment, reduced spending, and slower economic growth. Even hiring subsidies may not be enough to convince corporations to take on novice workers who have not yet acquired skills. In fact, most research finds that sharp increases in the minimum wage are linked to higher unemployment.

Another problem is that a one-size-fits-all minimum wage doesn't match local realities. Average wages vary widely between regions, states, and industries. Setting the same wage floor for an entire state—or for all 50 states—can be arbitrary. Even when exceptions are made, or when some cities adopt higher local minimum wages, these tweaks rarely solve the deeper mismatch across different industries and regions.

The main victims of a high minimum wage are inexperienced and unskilled workers, who are shut out of entry-level jobs. Even when they are willing to work for lower pay to gain experience, the minimum wage effectively bars them from doing so, denying them the chance to build skills and move up to higher wages later on.

Meanwhile, corporations that rely on basic tasks often respond by investing in automation—now more cost-effective than hiring at higher wages—or by outsourcing jobs to countries with lower labor costs. Both strategies accelerate domestic job losses.

Banning—or even limiting—robots through a "robot tax" is hardly practical. The idea of taxing advanced machinery to stimulate demand and wages for low-skill jobs may have more opponents than supporters. One major challenge lies in defining what qualifies as a robot for taxation purposes. Questions arise about the criteria for identification— whether it should be based on the presence of a CPU or other technical factors.

Comparative evidence further complicates the debate. For example, Germany, which has a higher per capita use of robots than the US, has lower income inequality. This suggests that the relationship between automation and economic disparity is not straightforward.

There are also concerns about the broader strategic implications of a robot tax. Critics argue that such a measure could weaken a nation's competitiveness on the global stage, particularly against authoritarian regimes that are aggressively investing in advanced robotics and artificial intelligence for both economic and military purposes. People cannot simply return to shovels and hammers for the sake of creating jobs, and high-tech industries cannot be taxed indiscriminately without considering geopolitical conse-quences. More viable alternatives are needed to address the economic challenges posed by automation while balancing domestic needs and global technological competition.

Tightening the screws: Small corporations should be spared excessive regulation

Congress remains hesitant to act too quickly, acknowledging the challenges small corporations face in adapting to higher wages or new hiring mandates. Large corporations often have the financial capacity to self-fund and transition smoothly to higher pay practices. Smaller firms, however, typically lack the resources to do so.

The abrupt imposition of strict pay standards could create serious difficulties for small corporations. Such a forced transition would require new processes, workforce retraining, revised supply chains, and even redesigned product lines to maintain profitability. For many small businesses, the only option would be to raise prices to offset higher labor costs. Since companies must account for all expenses—wages, taxes, and interest charges—failing to do so could result in chronic unprofitability, loan denials, insolvency, and ultimately bankruptcy.

This scenario could reduce national output, as large corporations would face less competition, potentially weakening innovation, efficiency, and long-term growth. Larger firms may also be less inclined to fill the gap left by bankrupt small businesses, especially in the short term. The result could be rising unemployment, economic disruption, and a slowdown in overall economic activity.

GOUVERNEMENT

Liberté
Égalité
Fraternité

France, at the heart of the EU, has a legally established minimum wage for workers. However, many individuals—particularly in suburban areas with marginalized communities—remain unemployed. This social exclusion, combined with the concentration of inactive populations in substandard public housing, often fuels periodic civil unrest and fosters conditions in which vulnerable individuals may be drawn to extremist ideologies.

France is trying to escape its status of the champion of regulations benefiting a few. However, the pace of reform is hindered by frequent street protests that often stall these changes. The government has so far failed to shift away from the long-standing paradigm of taxation, regulation, and redistribution pervasive across various economic sectors. France continues to trail in terms of economic agility and has yet to produce any major technology giants.

Deregulation post-1980

If the minimum wage cannot rise far above market levels, then it might as well be left to the market itself. This became increasingly clear amid the rising unemployment of the 1970s, when the illusion of government guidance began to unravel under the burden of excessive state intervention. Government influence, when too heavy, risks stifling the economy.

Today, the minimum wage is aimed primarily at preventing exploitation through extremely low wages. In real-dollar terms, it has declined since the 1970s, and it is not designed to lift overall wages or reduce income inequality between the wealthiest 10% and the poorest 10%.

Since the 1980s, supply-side economics has gradually supplanted demand-side economics. Supply-side policies were predicated on the belief that private corporations, rather than the government, were best positioned to assess product affordability, which in turn influences demand, investment, output, wages and employment. Supply-side economists viewed regulatory measures as burdensome, particularly for small businesses.

Today, governments tend to favor deregulation as a response to the post-war era's extensive governmental intervention in the economy. The removal of economic controls, including price ceilings, minimum wage mandates, and output regulations, is viewed as a more effective strategy to encourage investment by reducing the unpredictability associated with government actions.

This shift toward supply-side economics marked a significant turnaround, contributing to economic recovery after the stagnation experienced in the 1970s. Reverting to large government spending and demand-side strategies is now considered outdated, even though low-income wages have stubbornly plagued low-skill jobs.

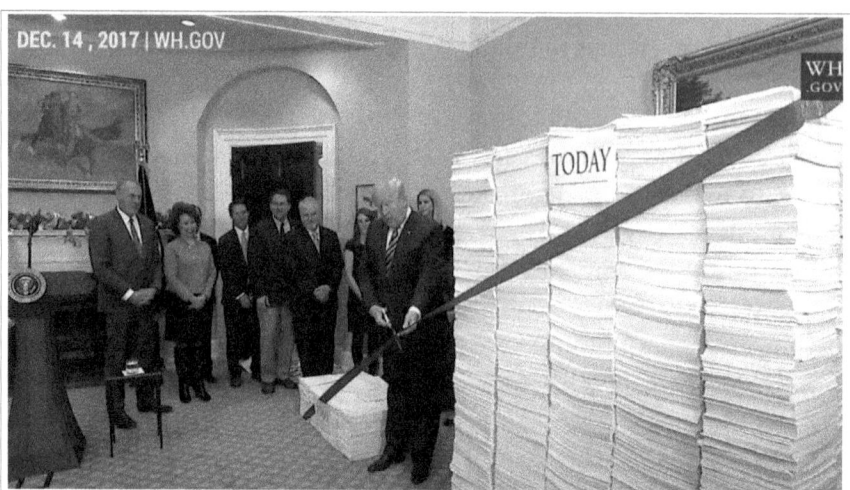

Regulations can impose heavy costs on businesses, requiring them to invest time and resources into compliance efforts. Small businesses, which make up roughly half of the economy, are disproportionately impacted because they have fewer resources to absorb these costs compared to larger corporations. Larger businesses, on the other hand, can more easily spread these expenses across a wider range of products and services, giving them a competitive edge. In fact, large corporations often support stringent regulations as a way to stifle competition from smaller companies. This is why they invest heavily in lobbying to shape regulations in their favor, turning the small pile of rules in 1960 into the regulatory leviathan of today, as shown in the picture.

Reducing regulations might be perceived as benefiting large corporations, but in reality, it can level the playing field for small businesses. In this context, President Trump's push for deregulation supported small businesses at the expense of larger corporations.

No, Government Handouts Are Not a Solution

US government hesitant to redistribute more

The US government has long implemented fiscal policies centered on taxation and redistribution to address income inequality. This includes programs such as the Supplemental Nutrition Assistance Program (SNAP), Medicaid, and other welfare initiatives designed to support lower-income individuals and families. These measures have helped lower-income households maintain a degree of economic parity with higher-income households.

The United States is not lagging behind other countries in this regard, as shown in the table below. Its total net social spending as a percentage of GDP—including public and private expenditures, the effects of direct taxes (income tax and social security contributions), indirect taxes on consumption tied to cash benefits, and tax breaks for social purposes—reflects a comprehensive approach.

The US is cautious about expanding its welfare programs, especially as other countries achieve better outcomes with fewer resources. The American welfare system is often criticized for its complex and cumbersome bureaucracy, which can prevent individuals from accessing the benefits to which they are entitled. Numerous studies indicate that while welfare programs are essential, they are poorly designed and fail to effectively reduce poverty.

Country	Total net social spending, % of GDP, 2019 ("*" if 2017)
France	30.1
USA	29.4*
Germany	25.4
Denmark	24.7
Italy	24.4
Japan	23.5*
Sweden	23.4
Canada	23.1*

Not too far: Welfare as a potential poverty trap

A key concern shaping welfare systems is their long-term effectiveness in combating poverty. Welfare is essential for providing temporary relief during economic downturns, but its success must also be evaluated by its ability to provide a lasting solution to poverty. To ignore its impact on poverty and view it instead as a permanent remedy for inequality through wealth redistribution is far from universally accepted.

In this sense, red flags are raised about the risk of welfare inadvertently fostering dependency rather than sustainably alleviating poverty. The concept of the "welfare trap" or "poverty trap" highlights this problem. It arises when welfare benefits approach the income from the lowest-paying jobs, discouraging individuals from seeking employment. As a result, welfare recipients may miss entry-level positions that could have led to better opportunities. This situation can trap individuals in dependency, idleness, participation in the underground economy, or even criminal activity—further hindering their economic progress.

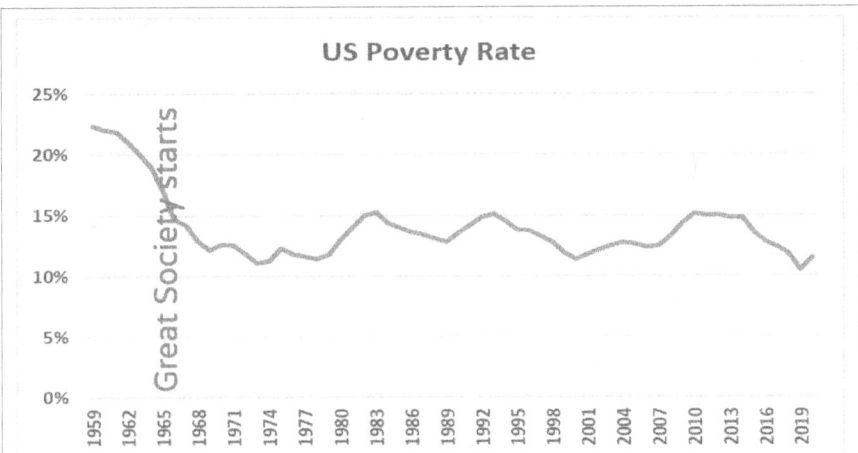

The Great Society programs, initiated in 1965, were designed as a comprehensive effort to combat poverty, with the goal of providing the underprivileged with the means to escape their fate. These programs were seen as a necessary supplement to existing public and faith-based welfare initiatives.

Interestingly, historical data shows that the US poverty rate was already declining before the Great Society programs began. Progress then stalled afterward, despite all the free money shoveled to the poor.

Throwing money at the problem has never ended poverty. It seems that poverty is a multifaceted issue that extends beyond mere financial constraints. Since then, the welfare programs have been amended numerous times, but never repealed. The ongoing debate in this realm has shifted toward restructuring these programs with a greater emphasis on workforce reintegration, rather than simply increasing the allocation of funds.

A negative tax for low-income jobs

In recent years, the US has shown a preference for income redistribution models that are linked to employment, as opposed to providing welfare benefits for staying idle at home and getting stuck in poverty.

A prime example of this approach is the Earned Income Tax Credit (EITC), a form of negative taxation for low-income earners. This system credits an amount of tax as "already paid" to the IRS, but only if the taxpayer has earned sufficient wages through employment. Welfare income does not qualify for triggering this negative tax. The structure of the EITC is designed to incentivize work: the more an individual works, the greater the potential reimbursement from the

IRS. The credit increases with earned income up to a certain threshold, after which it begins to phase out.

Critics warn that the EITC may lead some workers to accept lower-paying jobs. The alternative would be for them to demand higher wages to compensate for the loss of the EITC, despite their low skill levels—but would that be realistic? Simply put, the policy is designed to ensure that many individuals, especially those in lower-income brackets, find work, gain experience, and secure a minimum level of financial stability. For instance, in 2019, about 25 million taxpayers received over $63 billion in EITC, with the average amount being approximately $2,476. However, households with earnings above $56,000 were not eligible for the EITC.

The EITC, while valuable, is not a comprehensive solution and has inherent limitations. First, it is less effective in areas with few employment opportunities. Second, differences in state income tax rates and county sales taxes can diminish the benefits provided by the federal EITC. Third, fraudulent claims—in which individuals overstate their income to receive a higher credit—pose an ongoing challenge.

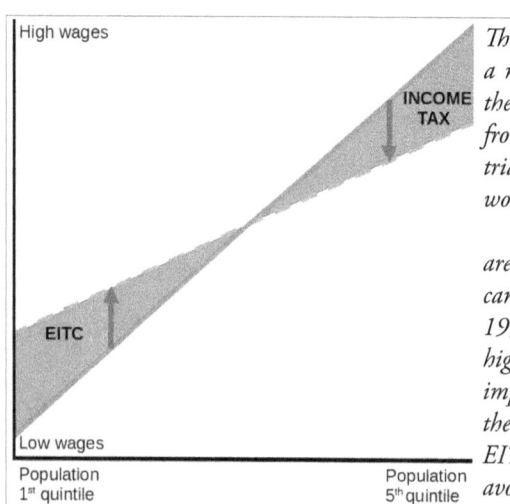

The EITC functions fundamentally as a mechanism for redistributing (as in the picture) the triangle "income tax" from high-income earners to the triangle "EITC" for low-income workers.

Implicitly, this suggests that there are limits to how much redistribution can be effectively implemented. The 1970s demonstrated that excessively high income taxation can negatively impact investment levels. Therefore, the scale of tax transfers through the EITC must be carefully calibrated to avoid adverse long-term economic effects, particularly regarding sustainable investment and long-term economic growth.

Welfare budgets should not overburden the economy

Expanding welfare or the EITC to include some of the middle class may be seen as a solution to stagnant incomes. Most transfer programs, however, were originally designed to redistribute wealth from the rich to the lowest income brackets—not to the middle class. This costly proposition faces serious practical difficulties and may not be feasible within current economic and policy frameworks.

The sustainability of government programs through borrowing and taxation also has its limits. Key economic principles dictate that rising deficits can fuel inflation. At the same time, high taxation levels can harm the economy by diverting funds from investment, reducing consumer demand, and impeding job creation. Eventually, excessive welfare spending can backfire and make everyone poorer.

The historical example of the Great Society programs initiated by President Johnson serves as a cautionary tale. These programs, designed to provide direct financial assistance to the poor, ultimately contributed to the economic crisis of the 1970s. This historical context forms the basis of the opposition to overly generous welfare budgets that could potentially overburden the economy.

Universal Basic Income (UBI) is a financial support model that offers unconditional payments to individuals, irrespective of their employment status. This concept has gained traction as a potential solution to the economic challenges and employment disruptions caused by the rapid advancement of robotic technology and automation in various industries. Various pilot programs, such as those conducted by Kela, the Social Insurance Institution of Finland, have explored the impact of UBI on societal aspects including employment. However, these trials have not conclusively demonstrated that UBI enhances social opportunities, suggesting the need for further research and experimentation.

The implementation of welfare programs and UBI raises important ethical and societal debates. One central question is whether the objective of such initiatives is merely to provide basic sustenance or to enable individuals to secure meaningful employment. Concerns have been raised that overly generous social security measures might inadvertently encourage a lack of motivation, contribute to the growth of the underground economy, or even foster criminal activities.

Many argue that all citizens, regardless of their economic status, should contribute to national endeavors. These include healthcare provision, food production, housing construction, and military support. The concept of freedom is often intertwined with the responsibility to contribute actively to the nation's development, especially in the face of challenges posed by autocratic governments abroad and global issues such as climate change. Robots can't do it all yet, and the nation can't rely on idleness to fill the ranks of the army while increasing the taxation burden on courageous workers paying for a generous UBI and clean energy for all.

Expanded benefit programs might set others back

To address inequality, some policymakers have proposed expanding welfare programs. Such benefits may include healthcare, college tuition, preschool, school meals, public transportation, and related services—extending well beyond conventional welfare provisions designed primarily for low-income groups and unemployed workers.

The first challenge with such handouts is that they can't satisfy everyone fairly within the same limited funding. Not all individuals need the same services, such as childcare or college classes. Implementing these extensive benefits could require reallocating funds from other vital services. Moreover, free services may exclude low-income households that slightly exceed the income eligibility thresholds.

A second criticism concerns the need for additional taxation or borrowing, which could slow economic growth, put pressure on the job market, and undermine wage levels, thereby negating the benefits.

Some individuals may find themselves doubly excluded: unable to access the government benefits they need because of their income level while also missing out on any gains from economic growth. This situation can create a sense of wage inequality and a feeling of being overlooked by welfare programs—potentially fostering disenchantment and support for more radical political alternatives.

Paperwork for subsidies can be dissuasive. According to the President's Biden White House website: "Administrative burdens make it harder for millions of individuals, families, and small businesses to receive government benefits and services for which they may be eligible. For some individuals, families or small businesses, these burdens —costs like the "time tax" required to learn about a program, fill out paperwork, assemble required documents, and schedule visits to government offices—completely prevent access to much-needed benefits. The Office of Information and Regulatory Affairs is working to [...] reduce those burdens."

This statement implies that one bureaucracy is attempting to fix another. A more effective approach could involve implementing tax reductions for low-income households without adding any additional bureaucracy.

The EU: Shrinking benefits over the last decades

In recent decades, some EU member states have implemented time limits on welfare benefits and raised the retirement age. Notable examples include the United Kingdom under Margaret Thatcher's leadership and Germany's "Agenda 2010" initiative. These countries successfully restructured their welfare systems, often drawing inspiration from the US model. Their reforms aimed to encourage employment, even in lower-paying jobs, as a means of stimulating economic participation and reducing dependency on state support.

By contrast, countries such as France and Italy have faced greater difficulties in reforming their welfare systems. The threat of mass protests has hindered reforms, creating hesitation in implementing major changes. Burdened by high tax rates and stringent regulations, these nations continue to grapple with economic stagnation.

The EU currently shows lower inequality than the US, as measured by the World Bank's Gini coefficient after taxes and transfers. However, this advantage may not last amid economic decline. European policymakers increasingly recognize that sustained growth is essential to meeting societal and governmental obligations. The EU is actively exploring ways to rejuvenate its economy, particularly by fostering high-quality jobs in the technology sector, even if this approach increases inequality—following the US model and as emphasized in Mario Draghi's study on excessive EU regulations.

The case of Sweden often arises in discussions about potential socialist models for the US. In reality, Sweden's postwar experience with a socialist-oriented economy went wrong, as author Johan Norberg explains. The country faced persistent inflation that ultimately led to an economic slump in the 1990s.

To recover, Sweden shifted toward a more market-oriented approach. Reforms included abolishing the wealth tax, capping property taxes, and reducing income taxes, among other measures. These changes came about a decade after similar reforms in the UK and ahead of countries like France and Italy, which still struggle with the challenges of state-owned enterprises and heavy regulation.

In 2019, public spending as a percentage of GDP placed Sweden between the UK and France (about 40% in the UK, 50% in Sweden, and 56% in France). This shows that Sweden's approach differs from both the more market-oriented UK model and the more socialist-leaning French model. Within the EU, France is the reference for a socialist economic system, not Sweden.

No, Education Alone Will Not Ensure Economic Mobility

Is it just about re-funding education?

Highly skilled jobs in the fields of engineering, plumbing, nursing, and other hard-to-fill positions have the potential to offer higher wages to workers. Therefore, shouldn't reinvesting in education reduce unemployment and inequality? Given the current state of schools, with broken windows and difficulties in attracting teachers due to low wages, shouldn't prioritizing education be a viable solution? By providing proper training, couldn't more graduates fill the high-pay job vacancies for AI developers, skilled welders or mechanical specialists?

The US education budget isn't small

The task of providing education is an ever-evolving process, and while there may be room for progress, previous reforms in both the US and the EU have been disappointing. There is no guarantee that a fresh round of reforms and increased budgets for education will improve the skill level of graduates.

The US budget for education is not relatively low when compared to other countries. It is reasonably ranked in comparison to the GDP of the OECD countries, even to the GDP of countries that have achieved better results and reduced inequality.

Given this budget context, critics of the US education system point to several issues: underperforming teachers shielded by strong unions, an emphasis on social sciences over technical and STEM (Science, Technology, Engineering, and Mathematics) training, and bloated administrations that absorb much of the funding. Many lawmakers also argue that vocational education and trade schools, which equip workers with essential job skills, should be a central priority for schools. Finally, there is the indiscipline of students from dysfunctional families, often influenced by juvenile gangs. If the root causes lie in broken families, then the solution may not be simply throwing more money at the school system.

Many countries have embraced school choice, allowing parents to select from public schools, charter schools, or, as in Belgium, free Catholic schools. This system often involves the selection of students, either for admission or for progression to the next grade, as well as the selection of teachers, sometimes without the constraints of inflexible tenure. By prioritizing student outcomes over teacher status, some competitive schools achieve better results than others, even with lower budgets. This demonstrates that success in education is not solely dependent on funding.

Learning from the experience of other countries

Germany could show the US how to retrain the unemployed through its voucher system for vocational programs in mechanics, electrical work, or other trades. These programs combine classroom education with hands-on work experience gained through corporate internships. Such an approach has proven effective in preparing individuals for skilled fields and enables them to return to the workforce.

Norway or Switzerland also have efficient education systems, which help to spare their citizens from growing inequality and diminishing low wages. Norway emphasizes STEM subjects, along with technical and entrepreneurial skills. Switzerland is successful as well with over 90% of 25-year-olds completing their technical training or college degree, making it the highest graduation rate in the world.

Sweden is also acclaimed for its education system and its high test results in international (PISA) evaluations. Sweden, like other European countries, but unlike most of the US, has a voucher system with public schools competing with private charter schools to enlist students, which exerts some control over school administrations. Parents and students selecting their school may be a factor of Sweden's success, although studies diverge about the relation between school choice and test scores in a country with a strong sense of discipline and patriotism.

These European countries may attribute their educational success to an emphasis on vocational training and workforce retraining, rather than simply increased education funding. However, this success remains only relative when it comes to non-EU migrants.

The idea of education as a cure for society's problems goes back at least to thinkers like John Locke (pictured), who envisioned the mind at birth as a "blank slate" that could be shaped through proper instruction.

In recent years, skepticism has grown over the belief that education alone can solve the world's problems. Critics of ever-expanding education budgets often cite evidence from "twins and adoption studies," which suggest that intelligence is partly genetic. These findings imply that education can enhance but not fundamentally alter intelligence.

Simply increasing school funding may not close the gap between average skill levels and the advanced capabilities demanded in technology, finance, and other white-collar professions. As a result, many argue that education and retraining should emphasize vocational training—as practiced in Germany and Switzerland—to create well-paid industrial jobs, rather than focusing only on college studies for high-end careers.

Education is slow to move people up the job ladder

US politicians are divided regarding the allocation of funds toward education and whether to adopt new pedagogical or administrative approaches to better equip students for lucrative career opportunities.

A first step would see every student finish high school, as it is free and public in the US. This first step is already a challenge. A second step would enroll everyone in community colleges, but not everyone wants it or can afford 2 years on school desks, both financially and mentally, let alone 4 years for a full college diploma. It is easier said than done to send more people to college.

An alternative approach would focus on retraining unemployed and low-skill workers without a high school diploma. But, if they failed in high school, will they succeed in retraining programs for manual studies? In the US, community college exists with a cheap tuition, but unemployed low-skill people aren't required or can't always attend these year-long evening classes. It is never obvious that retraining will bring results, as skilled welders and other well-paid jobs need years of on-the-job training after any kind of retraining.

Even after the enactment of a successful reform, there will be no immediate results but only in 10 or 20 years as students graduate through elementary to college in modernized schools. Fingers crossed, education and retraining will improve one day, and refunding will follow. But, this topic falls outside the scope of this present book focusing on economic policies.

Part 3

WILL NEW PROMISES SAVE

THE DAY?

Any plan to raise low wages will also have to face the impact of AI on jobs. AI is poised to reshape industries: research with faster drug discovery, manufacturing with affordable robots, transportation with driverless cars, and healthcare with improved medical diagnosis.

These advances raise a critical question: Will AI create jobs—or eliminate them? Already, some software developers have lost work to AI, forcing them into lower-paying roles or unemployment. Robots and AI systems are increasingly replacing people in routine tasks—and may soon take on more advanced ones, such as loading a dishwasher.

Protectionism Could Boost Low Wages

Return of tariffs aimed at raising US wages

Beginning in 2018 and intensifying in 2025, US tariffs were raised to rebalance trade with countries running industrial surpluses. For decades, foreign partners have flooded the US market with cheap imports, undermined local producers, encouraged multinationals to move jobs overseas, hollowed out supply chains in critical sectors, and suppressed the wages of American workers. These left-behind workers were the primary victims of international free trade, often told dismissively to "retrain" or "go to college"—even though higher education is not suited for everyone, as discussed in the previous section on education.

Domestic industries need some degree of protection from ruthless foreign competition. Without tariffs, a corporation like Tesla could barely compete with China's BYD, which benefits from an undervalued currency and cheap labor, including engineers who design and build low-cost robots. Rebalancing trade with tariffs could help restore low-skill jobs with better wages by re-industrializing the Rust Belt, reshoring factories of American corporations, pressuring foreign companies to open manufacturing facilities in the US, and re-establishing domestic supply chains that are critical for national security.

Cheap foreign labor may have been only a secondary cause of the decline in manufacturing jobs, with automation and robotics playing the primary role. Still, globalization has added downward pressure on low-income wages, and its effects cannot be dismissed as merely secondary. While tariffs may not restore every job lost since the 1970s —given that automation remains a dominant force—they could help low wages recover somewhat. And for workers at the bottom, every cent counts.

The globalization of trade may have been pursued with the best of intentions during the post–Cold War era, aiming to sway China and Russia toward democracy. The hope was to end all wars and boost economic growth, with wealthy countries focusing on high–value-added products made by increasingly skilled workers, while delegating the manu-facturing of cheap goods to developing nations.

After 2014, with the rise of nationalism under Xi Jinping and Vladimir Putin, the Western world came to realize that China and Russia were not on the path to becoming democratic partners. The geopolitical strategy of global trade had failed, and America's least-skilled workers paid the price of low-cost foreign competition.

Even foreign allies did not always play fair during the globalization era. Many accu-mulated trade surpluses with the US, exporting more than they imported in American goods. Meanwhile, these same partners ran trade deficits with China and maintained low military spending relative to GDP, despite their NATO commitments.

Trade agreements are now being recalibrated with the aim of reindustrializing the US while also strengthening Western unity in the face of the China–Russia alliance. This includes pressuring Germany and other allies to both strengthen their military and move away from growth strategies that rely heavily on exports to the US.

Tariffs at the risk of economic disturbance

US tariffs must be implemented strategically to avoid retaliatory measures aimed at hurting American workers. For this reason, the government may have to accept that some jobs will shift from China to friendly nations, but not necessarily return home—much to the disap-pointment of President Trump's supporters. This reliance is also neces-sary to maintain strong trade relationships with allied nations.

Tariffs must be applied cautiously to avoid derailing the economy. Ideally, buyers switch to domestic suppliers. But when alternative products or components are not available, consumers end up paying the tariffs. This affects the economy in two ways. First, tariffs siphon money away from private spending and investment, channeling it into government revenue—like any tax. Second, tariffs raise the prices of essential goods, creating inflationary pressure. Such pressure should force the Fed to raise interest rates, leading to a crowding-out effect that hurts the job market.

Applied recklessly, tariffs could backfire, hurting low-income workers even if some domestic jobs are created. Any middle-class wage gains from tariffs could easily be erased by a broader economic slowdown.

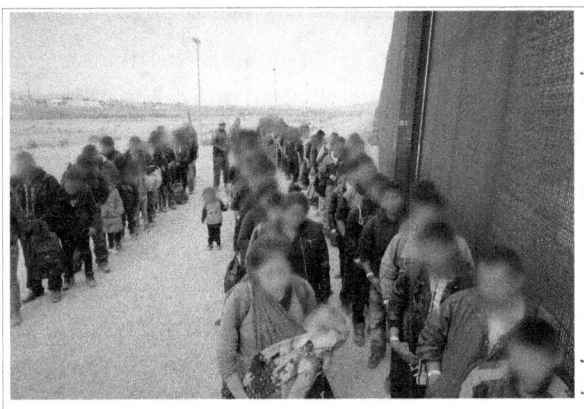

Do migrants take only the jobs that American workers avoid? Some argue yes, insisting that migrants benefit the economy and complement the work of other national laborers. Others disagree, pointing out that legal farmworkers —whether American or foreign—still hold more jobs than undocumented workers. They argue that migrants put downward pressure on wages, since many are willing to save just a few dollars a day, which goes much further in their home countries. For example, as purchasing power parity (PPP) studies show, savings can be worth several times more when used to build a house in places like Mexico or Guatemala. If wages are driven too low under pressure from undocumented labor and cheap imports, then only undocumented workers will take jobs such as harvesting vegetables, while saving their earnings for cheaper living costs abroad. Altogether, with limited economic data on undocumented migration to clarify its effects on the job market, many Americans want to see immigration restricted.

In the US, illegal immigration is expected to decline under President Trump due to the expulsion of undocumented migrants, as was also the case under Obama and previous presidents. These expulsions may help low wages recover somewhat.

In the EU, migrants were long welcomed with the expectation that they would work and raise families, helping offset population decline, support the economy, and fund social security systems. However, assimilation has not always been successful: unemployment remains high among some groups; idle migrants are sometimes viewed as costing more than they contribute to welfare systems; and they are often blamed for rising crime. EU voters are now pushing to restrict immigration in a manner similar to the US.

AI and Emerging Technologies Could Strengthen the Economy

Technology-driven productivity could create jobs

New revolutionary technologies could play a role in strengthening the job market, despite the apprehensions listed in Part 1. According to some pundits, advancements in artificial intelligence, quantum computing, biotechnology, and other emerging fields could catalyze rapid economic growth, and higher wages.

In economic terms, these technological innovations can enhance workforce efficiency, which directly contributes to *"productivity"*— defined as the ratio of output to input, such as revenue relative to capital investment. This metric, monitored by statistical agencies, serves as a key economic indicator. Productivity gains are tracked through corporate accounting data, economic surveys, and tax filings, and they encompass various aspects such as labor productivity, capital productivity, and material productivity. Such gains show how engineers and workers leverage new technologies to make investments in cheaper, better, and more innovative products more profitable.

Productivity gains have the potential to revitalize the economy. Lower production costs mean that essential goods, such as food, cars, and healthcare, become more affordable, leaving people with more disposable income. This additional income can be saved or spent on new products and services, stimulating demand in various sectors. Businesses, in turn, will respond by investing in innovations and offering new products and services, such as household robots, automated meal-preparation systems, and much more.

Productivity gains: Boosting GDP growth and economic well-being

As productivity increases, it drives overall GDP growth and encourages further investment in profitable ventures. Higher profitability can attract capital across various sectors, particularly in those that become more viable due to technological advancements. This, in turn, creates quality job opportunities and improves economic prospects for low-income workers.

Historical data suggests that when real GDP growth exceeds 3%, it can catalyze both employment growth and wage increases. A rapidly growing economy can also foster new business startups, expand employment opportunities, and reduce the cost of goods and services.

On the contrary, if productivity gains are insufficient and GDP growth stagnate below 2%, automation and robotics may keep on supplanting human workers and exert downward pressure on wages—a concern highlighted in the first section—while few new ventures and hiring projects are being funded.

The average GDP growth rate exceeded 4% during the 1950s and 1960s, but fell to 3% in the 1970s and 1980s and has hovered around 2% since 2000 (see chart: source BEA). Will today's promising technologies spark a recovery in GDP growth—lifting blue-collar wages—starting in 2024, despite inevitable downturns? Could this surge last longer than the dotcom boom of the 1990s, when GDP briefly surged above 4% for just a few euphoric years? This time, might technology be the transformative force that delivers lasting global prosperity?

AI could improve productivity across the board

Artificial Intelligence (AI) is considered a key solution to addressing the stagnation in productivity and modest GDP growth seen in recent decades. Similar to how personal computers and the internet boosted productivity in the past, AI has the potential to accelerate advancements. It can reduce costs in research-intensive industries, replace routine tasks previously handled by personal assistants, and enhance the profitability of investments by increasing efficiency across various sectors.

AI has the potential to enhance the productivity of highly skilled professionals across various industries, as discussed in the best-selling book *The Coming Wave* by Mustafa Suleyman. AI's capabilities span a wide range of applications, including refining text composition, automating initial drafts of software code, performing precise data analysis, and enabling robots to learn autonomously through trial and error. Its impact could be far-reaching, driving innovation in fields such as software development, pharmaceuticals, medical diagnostics, autonomous vehicles, quantum computing, biotechnology, advanced counseling and robotics software, and fraud detection in financial transactions, among others.

In the corporate sector, AI tools will primarily be developed within data centers operated by companies such as Amazon, Google, and Microsoft. AI research teams and consulting firms will use these resources to create advanced machine learning solutions for processing data, identifying patterns, and analyzing text, images, molecules, and algorithms. These AI specialists will help both large and small corporations design more cost-effective products and generate innovative new outputs.

Consumers will benefit from AI-optimized products designed to replace outdated and inefficient alternatives at lower costs. AI primarily focuses on optimizing existing processes rather than inventing entirely new products. For instance, AI could contribute to the development of new drugs, potentially reducing healthcare costs. It could also enhance agricultural productivity, making food more affordable, and enable cost-efficient production and transportation through robotics and autonomous vehicles. Furthermore, AI-powered services, such as affordable legal assistance, may become widely accessible, offering new opportunities for the general public.

Can AI and Technology Overcome All Obstacles?

Can AI boost economic growth quickly enough to create jobs?

It is difficult to predict whether AI will benefit job markets and wages. On the one hand, AI enthusiasts promise revolutionary changes, though their views may be overly optimistic due to vested interests. On the other hand, economists caution that future GDP growth driven by AI remains uncertain.

At present, AI does not directly generate widespread consumer demand or employment—aside from user-friendly applications like ChatGPT. This contrasts with the 1990s, when personal computers and the internet spurred job creation and mass consumer adoption. For now, AI remains primarily a corporate tool. Its short-term impact is more likely to be improved products or cost reductions in sectors such as pharmaceuticals, battery technology, and manufacturing. However, these innovations often replace existing products rather than create entirely new markets or job categories, as the internet once did.

In fact, AI is already contributing to job losses as companies use automation to streamline operations. AI tends to concentrate employ-ment in a small number of high-skill data center jobs while displacing medium-skill roles, such as content editors and software developers. Future automation may also impact drivers, cashiers, and other roles through the adoption of autonomous vehicles and other AI-powered systems. Meanwhile, transitioning displaced workers into trades like welding or electrical work is not easy, as these roles require years of training and hands-on experience—something not easily addressed through quick retraining programs.

These trends point to a fundamental challenge: productivity gains from AI depend on consumer demand. Companies are unlikely to invest in more efficient or lower-cost products if consumers lack the income to buy them. If wages fall faster than prices—or if job insecurity undermines consumer confidence—spending may stagnate. Unlike the Industrial Revolution, which addressed widespread demand from a growing middle class, today's AI-driven innovations—such as cancer treatments, service robots, or green batteries—often target niche markets, including retirees or affluent households upgrading to eco-friendly technologies.

So far, economists see little evidence that AI is significantly boosting overall productivity. Many warn that while AI may improve efficiency, the benefits are not widely shared. Instead, they often flow to a small number of individuals and corporations, while many workers face job insecurity and declining household incomes.

In the long term, AI holds significant potential, though its development is likely to be uneven. Yet many workers cannot afford to wait indefinitely for wage growth. At the same time, broader challenges—such as geopolitical tensions and climate change, which are often interconnected—may disrupt the global economy before AI-driven solutions can take full effect.

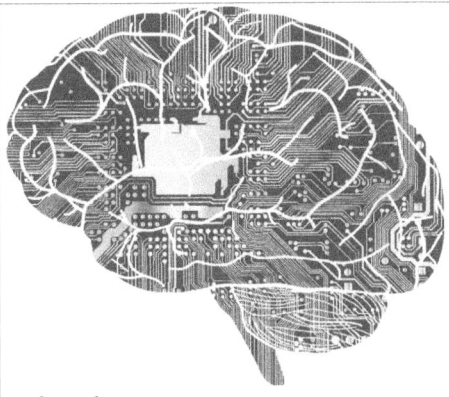

Will AGI (Artificial General Intelligence) replace workers and employees with smart robots?

Currently, no algorithms exist that can achieve the goal of human-like intelligence. AGI remains more of an aspirational concept promoted by startups seeking investment rather than an imminent reality. Despite advancements in AI, its capabilities are fundamentally limited to processing and learning from existing human-generated data without true independent reasoning or creativity.

This limitation implies that AI, as it stands today, cannot truly "think outside the box." This means it is unlikely to independently develop groundbreaking solutions to complex global challenges, such as drafting an economic policy to eliminate poverty or designing a viable nuclear fusion reactor.

AI and technology: A unifying force for the Western world?

The US must address domestic political polarization by demonstrating the tangible benefits of AI and technological advancements. A strong model of economic growth driven by these innovations can help reassure the public by creating jobs, increasing wages across all sectors, and potentially reducing income inequalities.

Beyond domestic considerations, AI and technology must also play a role in strengthening ties with key allies, including Europe, Japan, and potentially the Global South. It is not sufficient for the US to focus solely on producing superior products and exporting them worldwide. Relying on exports alone to overcome economic challenges may not be a sustainable strategy, as it could weaken allies who depend on US trade.

Technology must also save the climate

AI and other new technologies could make all kinds of products more affordable—including green ones. This would support economic growth while also advancing sustainability goals. The green transition could move forward without slowing productivity and without relying on punishing carbon taxes to guide the economy in that direction.

Currently, AI and robotics are placing strain on power grids. To keep up, some major AI companies are investing in nuclear power. It is still unclear whether this will make nuclear energy more popular or simply take resources away from other green energy efforts. At the same time, AI firms are working on more efficient computer chips, but these will take years to spread widely.

The world can't afford to chase AI-driven growth while delaying the green transition and relying on fossil fuels. Sustainable development isn't optional. AI and new technologies need to help speed up, not slow down, the shift to a greener future.

Compensating the Global South for green transition efforts

In addition to boosting their own economic growth, Western countries must also provide financial support to help developing nations transition to greener economies. The Global South, which faces significant climate-related challenges, has expressed concerns about the impacts of global warming—largely driven by emissions from industrialized nations over the past century.

A broader commitment from wealthier countries is essential. This includes offering compensation in the form of affordable access to green energy for countries in the Global South, which may not directly benefit from AI advancements yet are disproportionately affected by climate change.

Part 4

MONETARY ECONOMICS,

NOT POLITICS

AI could help design cheaper, better products with fewer workers—but it's unclear whether this would generate much growth and many new jobs.

What is needed is a new economic framework supported by a fresh approach to money —much like how the Industrial Revolution was partly fueled by the introduction of paper banknotes alongside scarce precious-metal coins, enabling the purchase of new products. This kind of innovation puts money directly into consumers' hands, generating excitement and paving the way for an entirely new economy to emerge. Studying the history of money and understanding how monetary systems have evolved could inspire the next major economic transformation.

Monetary Changes Have Repeatedly Bypassed Politics

AI has the potential to boost productivity, but is it enough to steer the economy toward higher wages for the middle class for meaningless consumerism, while ignoring the risks of climate change? However, achieving this goal may require innovative approaches, such as rethinking product taxation and exploring new monetary strategies.

Monetary economics presents an opportunity for driving change. The idea of financing new ventures by modifying the existing monetary system is not novel. Historically, monetary systems have demonstrated remarkable adaptability, evolving from physical assets like silver and gold coins to today's digital representations of money in bank accounts. This evolution underscores the flexibility of monetary frameworks in responding to economic needs.

As in the books below, the next stage of monetary evolution could involve alternative currencies aimed at accelerating the velocity of money within a distinct economic market—separate from traditional and informal economies. This approach could unlock new opportunities for economic activity, lift all wages and contribute to tackling contemporary economic and environmental challenges.

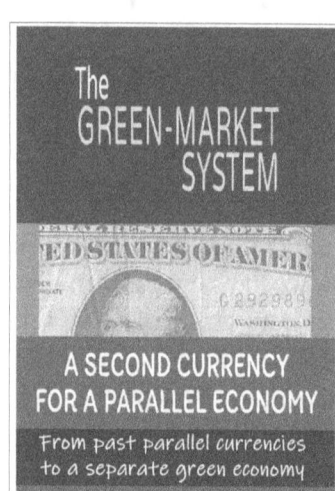

FREE: FOR A PARALLEL GREEN ECONOMY:

(Extract of the "History of Money for Understanding Economics")

For readers with some background in economics, the book "The Green-Market System" explores historical monetary shifts and parallel markets. Building on these examples, it proposes a revised monetary framework designed to launch a parallel economy—one that creates jobs and generates alternative income without being burdened by excessive taxes and regulations.

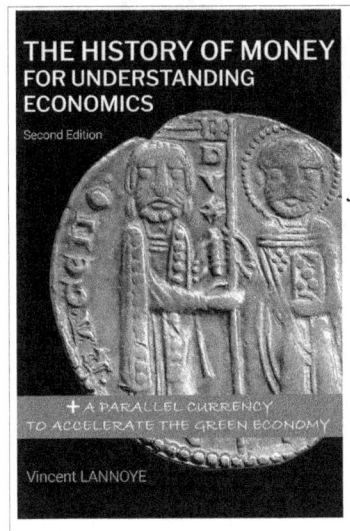

FROM THE MUTATIONS OF THE MONETARY SYSTEM TO A PARALLEL CURRENCY:

The accessible book "The History of Money for Understanding Economics" delves into the evolution of the monetary system from its inception to the advent of digital currency, exploring its impact on historical events.

The book poses intriguing questions, such as whether the Roman Empire failed to industrialize (and survive) due to its inability to invent a new form of currency to finance new industries. In contrast, it highlights how Great Britain successfully industrialized in the 18th century by introducing banknotes made of inexpensive paper, which played a crucial role in financing its Industrial Revolution.

Looking ahead to the 21st century, the book explores whether the modern world might need another transformation in its monetary system to address persistent inequalities and the challenges posed by the Green Revolution, ultimately making politics a mere epiphenomenon of macroeconomics.

BIBLIOGRAPHY

The complete bibliography can be found in:
Lannoye, Vincent. The History of Money for Understanding Economics. 2015

ORIGIN OF ILLUSTRATIONS

[0] Cover: Museum der Brotkultur, Ulm - Flemish painter 17th century, Public domain, via Wikimedia Commons [1] Kurt Kaiser, CC0, via Wikimedia Commons [4] Courtesy of Iliya Pitalev, via Wikimedia Commons [5] Created with chatGPT	[7] Author's collection, which includes many copies. [8] Courtesy of DimiTalen, via Wikimedia Commons [9] Courtesy of www.gouvernement.fr [10] Courtesy of Kremlin.ru [11] Courtesy of Senate Democrats [12] Courtesy of Gage Skidmore, via Wikimedia Commons [13] public domain.